RICHARD MAGGS

THE COMPLETE BOOK OF AGA KNOW-HOW

Absolute Press

First published in Great Britain in 2004 by
Absolute Press, an imprint of
Bloomsbury Publishing Plc

Absolute Press
Scarborough House
29 James Street West
Bath BA1 2BT England
Phone 44 (0) 1225 316013
Fax 44 (0) 1225 445836
E-mail info@absolutepress.co.uk
Website www.absolutepress.co.uk

Reprinted 2006, 2008, 2010 (twice), 2012

Publisher Jon Croft
Commissioning Editor Meg Avent
Designer Matt Inwood

A catalogue record of this book is available from the British Library

ISBN 9781904573234

Printed and bound in Italy by Printer Trento

Bloomsbury Publishing Plc
50 Bedford Square, London WC1B 3DP
www.bloomsbury.com

CONTENTS

INTRODUCTION

The Aga is not only the best cooker in the world, it is also the simplest, utilising the principle of heat storage, the oldest known form of cooking. You don't have to re-learn how to cook, nor abandon your favourite recipes and cookbooks. You simply need to understand that there are many easy Aga techniques available for you to enjoy. These will save you time and work, give consistently good results and even make washing up easier. The Aga will quite simply transform your cooking and lifestyle. After all, the Aga was designed from day one to be the easiest cooker to use.

The Aga was invented in 1922 by Dr Gustaf Dalén, the eminent Swedish physicist and Nobel Prize winner. When he built a new house in Stockholm for himself and his wife, he looked for a cooker which was capable of every cooking method – baking, boiling, braising, frying, grilling, roasting, simmering, steaming, stewing and toasting. He demanded a cooker that would be able to do all these things to perfection with the minimum of attention. After failing to find such a stove, he set himself the goal of designing a cooker that would provide perfect cooking, which was easy to use and incorporated totally automatic heat control:

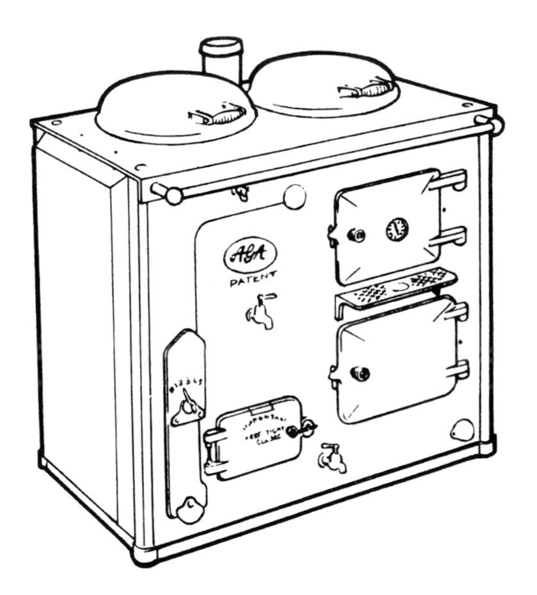

'I have now, with the help of my collaborators, constructed a kitchen range which I think meets rather exacting demands on convenience and low running costs.'
Dr Gustaf Dalén

TEN ESSENTIAL FUNCTIONS, ONE OUTSTANDING COOKER (DALEN'S ORIGINAL BRIEF)

Baking Like a traditional baker's brick oven, the Aga Roasting and Baking Ovens provide all-round, consistent heat to create authentically cooked pastry and light-as-a-feather sponge cakes. Fruit cakes turn out deliciously moist and perfectly level, and home-made bread is well-risen.

Boiling Water boils faster on an Aga than on a conventional cooker. The Aga Boiling Plate cooks fresh green vegetables so rapidly that they retain more of their natural vibrant colour, flavour and nutrients.

Braising The legendary Aga Simmering Oven is perfect for the long, slow cooking of meltingly tender braised dishes, developing intense flavours whilst wonderfully tenderising foods by gently breaking down their fibres.

Frying You can create really crisp battered and breadcrumbed fried fish and chicken using the large heat reserves found in the Aga Boiling Plate. Use the floor of the Roasting Oven to cook messy and strong-smelling foods to ensure crisp, non-greasy results every time.

Grilling The special cast-iron Aga grill pan is perfect for cooking succulent steaks, chops and cutlets on the fierce Aga Boiling Plate or on the floor of the Roasting Oven. It's the nearest thing to an authentic charcoal grill, which means the outside of the meat is quickly seared, driving the natural juices of the meat towards the centre, sealing in the flavour and reducing shrinkage.

Roasting The cast-iron construction of the Aga Roasting Oven seals in all the juices ensuring amazingly moist roasts and wonderful crackling. The even radiation of all round heat means exceptionally even cooking so it is unnecessary to baste a joint, and shrinkage will be minimal.

Simmering The Aga Simmering Oven is kind to food and the forgiving heat ensures there is no need for frantic last-minute preparations when entertaining. Much of a complicated meal can be prepared ahead and left to keep hot without deterioration. Overnight and gentle slow cooking is a special forté of this oven.

Steaming Use the Aga Simmering Oven to steam fish and hams to tender perfection. Delicious sweet and savoury puddings are cooked here with absolutely no need for topping up. Vapour lock in all the flavour and nutrients when cooking potatoes, root vegetables and rice.

Stewing The gently persistent heat of the Aga Simmering Oven helps make delicious and succulent stews and casseroles. These can be slow-cooked for many hours, giving you time to attend to other dishes or simply to relax.

Toasting The Aga even makes its own special type of toast: Aga toast, with its hallmark lattice branding. Use the wire toaster on the Boiling Plate to make perfect toast that is deliciously crisp on the outside, yet light and fluffy on the inside.

1. HOW THE AGA WORKS

An Aga is easier to use than a conventional cooker if you follow a few simple, basic rules.
In particular, the fully automatic heat control removes the need for complicated knobs and dials, and makes cooking simplicity itself.

I've put together seven basic principles; quickly adopted, these will soon turn you into a complete Aga expert. Everything becomes extremely easy when you just understand how the Aga works.

ALWAYS READY FOR USE

If you saw your Aga as it was being built in your kitchen you may have noticed the large castings which make up the ovens, hotplates and other heat-accumulating components. These solid castings are kept permanently at a very high temperature and act as heat stores, locking away large quantities of heat from an unusually small and efficient heat source. Originally this was solid fuel, but these days it is more commonly a small gas or oil burner, or has small electric elements. The stored heat in the Aga is contained by a large quantity of highly efficient insulation material that is carefully packed around the castings and this completely fills the inside of the outer case of the cooker.

Special heat conducting plates within the cooker distribute the heat in exactly the correct proportions to different parts of the cooker so that all cooking stations are maintained at pre-set temperatures for every possible cooking function. Once all the different parts have received their full amount of heat, it takes only a little fuel to maintain these temperatures. The heat source automatically drops down to a low setting – a mere thread of heat – to ensure everything is always maintained ready for immediate use. You never have to wait for an oven to heat up, and 'always ready' is a principle that is at the heart of what makes the Aga the best-loved cooker in the world.

AUTOMATIC TEMPERATURE CONTROL

When you start cooking, some of the stored heat is used up and the thermostat automatically responds to increase the heat source to replenish it. After a period of recuperation the thermostat returns the heat source to its low setting. The user therefore has no adjustments to make: the thermostat takes care of it all automatically. All Aga cookers that are still running on their original fuel from new, will continue to run at optimal thermal efficiency and are totally automatic in their control. This has been the case since the first Aga cooker was sold in 1929 and many original cookers are still in daily use. The heat indicator on the front of the Aga shows whether the cooker as a whole has the correct amount of stored heat within it. After fine-tuning the thermostat control for the first few days after installation, the cooker should be run so that the mercury sits on or about the black line in the silver section of the heat indicator. Once the correct setting has been determined, the controls never require any further adjustment on the part of the user. As cooking commences, the mercury will fall slightly; this is normal, and the thermostat will automatically replace the heat used. The heat indicator should only be referred to first thing in the morning or after a period of many hours with no cooking.

FOOD TASTES BETTER ON AN AGA

Food tastes better when cooked in an Aga because of the way it cooks. Conventional ovens generate heat from internal gas flames or electric elements, causing uneven cooking and the inevitable drying out of food. The Aga ovens use radiant heat from all sides evenly and gently – a far superior way of cooking. The cast-iron construction provides constant temperatures that seal the surface of foods quickly without drying them out. Stored heat is transmitted to the Roasting Oven from every angle giving an all round even temperature which provides succulent roasts which are attractively browned, and meltingly tender. When you want food crisp, such as for wonderful roast potatoes and fantastic pork crackling, the really hot Roasting Oven also makes this a simple matter. The built-in humidity control also ensures that food dries out less and basting and protecting are virtually unnecessary. The gentle persistent heat of the Aga Simmering Oven in particular renders all kinds of foods absolutely delicious and wholesome. When you cook on an Aga you start to enjoy cooking more and the consistent results mean you feel more confident to try more adventurous recipes.

'The secret of the fullest success of the Aga cooker lies in the knowledge of making the utmost use of the various parts of which it is composed.'
Ambrose Heath, Good Food on the Aga, 1933

THE AGA HOTPLATES

On the Aga there are no knobs or switches to turn or forget, no burners to light, no waiting and no low gas settings to blow out. The two main temperatures you need on a hob – extremely hot for rapid cooking and bringing things to the boil, and gentle, temperate heat for slow boiling, heating milk and making delicate sauces – are always available immediately. Together the two large hotplates will accommodate six to eight saucepans. Thus every temperature in between the two extremes is possible by simply adjusting the amount a pan is on a hotplate for infinitely variable heating.

THE BOILING PLATE

The left-hand hotplate is the hottest part of the Aga and in fact is the fastest domestic hotplate in the world. At full temperature it is approximately 600°F. The intense heat is spread evenly over the whole surface and by using utensils with thick bases that are perfectly flat its performance is amazing. Use its punchy bite for boiling kettles quickly, for heating up food before finishing cooking elsewhere on the cooker and for rapidly boiling green vegetables to maintain their bright colour. It is also perfect for making toast, grilling, deep fat frying, stir-frying and bringing preserves quickly to a rolling boil. Keep the lid down at all times when not in use to conserve heat.

TOASTING

Use the wire Aga toaster to make perfect Aga toast. Cooking with the insulated lid down produces toast crisp on the outside and fluffy within; leaving the lid up gives a crisper centre. To prevent any danger of sticking, always pre-heat the Aga toaster on the hotplate before making toast and clean only with the wire brush. To prevent fouling the hinge, place the toaster on the Boiling Plate with the handle to the left. Always keep your hotplates free of toast crumbs after toasting, by using the wire brush supplied with your Aga. Absolutely clean hotplates are essential to ensure efficient heat transfer to saucepans. As an alternative, toast may also be made directly on the Simmering Plate whilst boiling a kettle on the Boiling Plate at the same time. For delicious Melba toast, use medium-sliced bread cooked directly on the Simmering Plate. Cool and then place on a board. With a sharp serrated knife de-crust and cut each slice horizontally into two thin halves. Turn these over and finish off for a few minutes on a tray low down in the Roasting Oven. To cook poppadums, place them one at a time directly on the Boiling Plate with the lid lowered for just a few seconds, turning several times. Watch carefully so they don't burn.

GRILLING

Use the Aga grill pan to grill meat on the same principle as a charcoal grill. The intense heat from the Boiling Plate drives the natural juices of the meat towards the centre, sealing in the flavour and reducing shrinkage. Pre-heat a clean and dry cast-iron grill pan on the Boiling Plate for three or four minutes to absorb the full amount of heat ready for cooking. Brush the ridges with a little fat from the side of the meat and then place the meat on the ridges. Alternatively, lightly oil the food, but never the pan. Press the steak down so it makes good contact and cook for 1-2 minutes a side for rare, or if you prefer, a minute longer each side for medium. Apart from steaks, chops and cutlets, meaty types of fish such as fresh swordfish, tuna, salmon and marlin also work well using this technique, together with some shellfish such as scallops. Brush the fish very lightly with oil before cooking. Once the food has been added to the pan, alternatively transfer the pan to the floor of the Roasting Oven to finish cooking. Splashes and smells will then be removed from the oven by the integral oven venting system.

THE SIMMERING PLATE

The right-hand hotplate is kept at a safe, gentle, controlled temperature. It is ideal for foods where the fierce heat on the Boiling Plate would be too strong. It is perfect for gently heating milk and making sauces – even difficult ones – and for continuing to simmer vegetables before draining and finishing to steam in the Simmering Oven (*see* page 31). Slow frying is done to perfection here and even the gentle frying of eggs is easy. Eggs may also be gently poached and scrambled using a suitable pan. Keep the lid down at all times when not in use to conserve heat.

THE INTEGRAL GRIDDLE

Pancakes, scones and breads The Simmering Plate is also perfect for the direct cooking of batter mixes and traditional griddle scones and breads. Lightly grease the plate with a little cooking oil on a piece of kitchen paper before using. If your Simmering Plate is a little hot, raise the lid for a few minutes while you make the scone mixture. Pour on a batch of drop scones – by the time you have poured the last one, bubbles will have appeared on the first one indicating it is ready for turning. Re-grease the plate between batches. Spread thinner crêpe batter on the Simmering Plate using the back of a spoon before turning with a palette knife.

Toasted sandwiches These can be cooked, four at a time, directly on the Simmering Plate or on a piece of Bake-O-Glide. Lower the lid to speed the cooking and turn after 3-4 minutes. Easy cheese on toast for one will toast and melt in the centre of the hotplate with the lid closed. Tortillas and wraps are also easily prepared here.

Fat-free Cooking A delicious fat-free fried egg can be cooked in the centre of a piece of Bake-O-Glide with the insulated lid closed.

Popcorn Maker Store your un-popped popcorn in the freezer for the fluffiest results. Place a rectangular piece of Bake-O-Glide on the Simmering Plate and add a tablespoon of popcorn. Close the lid and only open when all the popping has finished. Pick up opposite corners of the Bake-O-Glide to catch all the corn in the valley which forms and pour into a serving bowl to dress with butter and a little salt or caster sugar.

THE WARMING PLATE

This useful extra feature on 4 oven cookers is great for keeping food warm and for serving from. It also acts as a useful 'parking' area when taking large joints and birds out of the oven to rest. It can also be used for keeping meat and poultry hot whilst carving in the kitchen. Syrups can be warmed, chocolate melted and flour pre-warmed for bread-making. As well as for warming gravy boats and vegetable tureen lids without their handles becoming too hot to lift, I find it especially useful for drying piping bags and nozzles and awkward metal items fresh from the dishwasher. The heat is even gentle enough to dry food processor bowls and plastic containers safely. It also keeps the toast rack and teapot warmed and is great for gently warming a jar of jam to make it easy to spread on a cake.

THE TOP PLATE

The area of the enamelled top plate in front of and between the two closed lids is perfect for making and keeping hot delicate sauces such as Hollandaise and Béarnaise. Protect the enamel with a piece of kitchen paper while whisking the sauce to a perfect conclusion. Dishes of melted butter for dressing vegetables can similarly be kept hot until wanted. If the telephone rings, a mug of coffee can even be kept from going cold here. Flour may be warmed for bread-making and chocolate and frostings melted for cakes.

Before exploring the Aga ovens, to get the best out of an Aga it is important to understand some basic principles. Grasp and follow these and you will become an expert Aga cook overnight.

THE SEVEN PRINCIPLES OF AGA KNOW-HOW

1. THE 80:20 PRINCIPLE
2. THE HEAT ZONE PRINCIPLE
3. THE PARTIAL OFFSET PRINCIPLE
4. THE LIDS DOWN PRINCIPLE
5. THE 7 MINUTE PRINCIPLE
6. THE START AND TRANSFER PRINCIPLE
7. THE SHIELDING PRINCIPLE

1. THE 80:20 PRINCIPLE

On a conventional cooker you typically cook 80% of your food on the top of the cooker, and turn on an oven specially to cook 20% of your food, for example, when baking a cake or roasting meat. With the Aga, the reverse should be followed. The hot ovens, full of stored heat, are always available for instant use. Absolutely no pre-heating is required, so cook 80% of your food in the ovens, and only 20% of your food on the hotplates – typically these are things which take a short period of time. This is the Golden Rule of Aga Cooking. When you learn of all that is possible in the Aga ovens you will see why the Aga is such a labour-saving cooker. This principle not only conserves the stored heat, but keeps you and the kitchen cool, and ensures that food actually requires less supervision and makes little or no mess on the top of the cooker.

'On no account should the idea be formed that the Simmering Oven is merely a hot cupboard for keeping things warm. If this is done, a great many of the special advantages of the Aga will be missed.'
Ambrose Heath, Good Food on the Aga, 1933

Here are some of the main oven cooking techniques which aren't immediately obvious to new users when they first start using an Aga:

LOW TEMPERATURE 'HOB COOKING' IN THE SIMMERING OVEN

Oven Vegetable Steaming All potatoes and root vegetables should be started on the top of the cooker and then drained and finished by steaming in the oven.

Oven Rice and Pasta Rice can cook to perfection in water or stock in the oven. Pasta once brought to the boil can finish cooking in a covered pan in the oven.

Softening Onions and Garlic Onions and garlic can be heated in butter and oil on the Boiling Plate for just a minute, being stirred a few times, and then the pan transferred to the oven for 20-30 minutes to soften and become tender. Return the pan to the hotplate to drive off any moisture that collects and brown if necessary, before proceeding with your recipe.

Sauces Once milk, stock or other liquid has been incorporated into a roux, transfer the covered saucepan to the oven to finish cooking.

Steam Sweet and Savoury Puddings After an initial period of 30 minutes' slow boiling on the Simmering Plate, sponge and suet mixtures, including Christmas puddings, can be transferred in the pan to the oven to finish steaming.

Long Slow Simmering Once started, all pans needing gentle simmering should be transferred to the oven to finish cooking and no stirring will be necessary. Prolonged simmering on the Simmering Plate should be avoided.

HIGH TEMPERATURE 'HOB COOKING' IN THE ROASTING OVEN

Oven Shallow Frying Shallow fry in a container on the floor of the oven. For example, instead of cooking sausages in a frying pan on the top of the cooker, do this in the oven and you will obtain better results with no mess. If browning meat for a casserole, this can also be done in a full size Aga roasting tin on the floor of the oven. Turn the floured meat every few minutes and a batch will soon be finished. Be careful not to over-crowd the tin to prevent the meat from steaming rather than browning.

Oven Contact Grilling The cast-iron grill pan can be used on the floor of the oven. Pre-heat this first on the Boiling Plate and then once the food is added, transfer to the floor of the oven where it will continue to cook with all mess and fumes contained and removed. The pan can alternatively be pre-heated on the floor of the oven but should be finally heated on the Boiling Plate before use to get it as hot as possible for the best results.

Oven Pre-heating Empty utensils can be pre-heated in the oven before use, providing they do not have wooden or plastic handles. For the hottest results, once pre-heated, always move an empty utensil to the Boiling Plate for a minute or two before use to finally get it to the highest temperature possible, before commencing grilling or stir-frying. Use Aga gauntlets or pan handle covers to protect yourself from hot handles.

2. THE HEAT ZONE PRINCIPLE

You don't *set* the heat with an Aga: you *find* it. By selecting the correct position in or on the cooker the food will cook to perfection, with the cooker temperatures being automatically adjusted by the thermostat. There is a strong gradient of heat from the top of the Roasting Oven to the bottom of the Simmering Oven. Different zones in the hot ovens have different cooking characteristics suitable for different purposes. No special recipes are required, just the simple expedient of knowing where to position the food in the cooker. There are several simple anchor points of reference which are useful to know. For example, the normal fast roasting times in standard cookbooks can be followed (so many minutes per lb /450g, etc.), once you know that the meat or poultry should be placed in an Aga roasting tin and this hung on the lowest set of runners in the Roasting Oven.

RADIANT HEAT: KIND TO FOOD

The heat in the Aga ovens is quite simply kind to food – forgiving almost – and you can largely forget about being tied to temperatures. Simply select the position in the cooker which will give the most suitable cooking environment. Certainly there is hot air in the ovens, but it is the invisible infra-red light radiated from the heavy oven castings that cooks and browns the food so deliciously.

THE GRID SHELF 'HOME' POSITION

Remember the Aga is *your* Aga, and you will want to customise it *your* way, to suit *your* lifestyle. For instance, I usually like to keep a grid shelf on the floor of the Roasting Oven, as I like to keep the rest of the oven free to be able to slide in tins and shelves at other levels. For new users, if you're not sure where to cook something, placing it on the grid shelf on the floor of this oven is a good general catch-all. Here you have a good hot oven to get your food cooked, but you are placing the food as far away as possible from the aggressive browning at the top of the oven and away from the direct heat of the floor of the oven. It is a simple matter then to remove the grid shelf quickly when the floor of the oven is wanted for direct cooking, for example, a quick pizza. Another position popular with some owners is to keep a grid shelf on the lowest set of runners in the Roasting Oven. There is a trick to learn to make removing the grid shelves easy. With the shelf in the oven, lift it up skywards from the front and while still pulling it upwards, slide it out of the oven. To insert it, once on the oven runners tilt the shelf down slightly so that the up-stands at the back of the shelf lift over the anti-tilt lugs as the shelf is inserted. When the shelf is pushed back the full way, the front of the shelf will drop down level again. Note that the top set of runners do not have anti-tilt lugs so a hot shelf is particularly easy to insert and remove here when you quickly want it out of the way.

3. THE PARTIAL OFFSET PRINCIPLE

People often wonder how to adjust the rate of cooking on the hotplates. With the Aga, positioning is everything, and with good utensils every rate of cooking is possible on the hotplates by adjusting the position of the pans on the hotplates. One of the best features of the completely flat top of the Aga is that once a pan has come to the boil, you can lift and partially offset pans so that you can adjust the rate at which foods cook exactly. If you use pans with heavy bases, as featured on all Aga cookware, a pan with only as little as a third making contact with hotplate will conduct the heat across the whole of the base of the pan. In this way you can have at least six pans on the top of the cooker if necessary. Pans with poor bases will not enable you to make the most of this extremely useful feature.

Deep Fat Frying Pre-heat the oil on the Simmering Plate, then move to the Boiling Plate to reach the desired temperature – use a frying thermometer. Partially offset the pan to prevent it over-heating, returning the pan fully to the Boiling Plate as necessary to maintain the temperature.

Perfect Simmering The best place on the Aga for proper simmering is the Simmering Oven. Apart from a few exceptions (meringues, rich fruitcakes, lemon curd, etc.), food should always be first brought to temperature elsewhere on the cooker. Pans that have started on the rapid Boiling Plate will continue to boil slowly for a few minutes on the Simmering Plate, e.g. a casserole or root vegetables, before being transferred to finish off in the Simmering Oven. If you are using a casserole that isn't flameproof and which wouldn't withstand the heat of the hotplates, heat this through for 20-30 minutes on the grid shelf on the floor of the Roasting Oven until it is gently bubbling. Then transfer to the Simmering Oven for the food to be gently coaxed to perfection.

As a general rule, pans should be covered with a tight-fitting lid when cooking in the Simmering Oven. However, if you want to reduce a sauce whilst it is cooking – a Bolognaise or Ragù sauce, for example – leave this to simmer uncovered in the Simmering Oven and over several hours it will cook and thicken with perfect results and no splashing. A cheat's risotto may be started off on the Simmering Plate and then left to finish off uncovered in the Simmering Oven, where the rice will absorb the stock as it cooks. Paellas may be similarly finished off here without the usual attention required.

The Aga Simmering Oven is perfect for family cooking and for entertaining, even with an ambitious menu. If guests are late, the food will happily keep safe in the Simmering Oven without burning or spoiling. When you have an Aga, you enter the world of stress-free entertaining.

4. THE LIDS DOWN PRINCIPLE

The insulated lids trap the heat of the Aga when you are not using them. They should always be kept down, between using the hotplates, even if this is only for a few minutes. If you follow the Golden Rule of cooking as much as possible in the ovens and as little as possible on the hotplates, you will find you never run out of heat. Whenever you need to use the hotplates, lift the lid confidently and the perfect temperatures you require will then always be ready and waiting for you.

Banish Heat Loss Forever Over-use of the hotplates, and prolonged use of the Simmering Plate in particular, is the main reason for excessive heat loss. During cooking it is normal for the mercury in the heat indicator to fall slightly; this is part of the design of a heat storage cooker. However, there are large reserves of heat stored in the heavy castings to cope with cooking a large and ambitious meal. After a demonstration where I might cook 15-20 different things, the Aga will still have plenty of heat at the end, because the cooker has been used in the way it was designed to be used. Reserve the hotplates for when you really need them and they will then offer you their full store of heat.

Rapid Heat Recuperation Of the two hotplates, the Boiling Plate recuperates the fastest after use. This is because it is situated directly above the heat source. Keeping the Simmering Plate lid down minimises heat loss from the Roasting Oven. When cooking a lot of food requiring a high temperature in the Roasting Oven, such as for a roast meal, avoid over-using the Simmering Plate. Reserve it for tasks where its gentler heat is essential such as when heating milk and making sauces. In this case, when continuing to boil vegetables for a few minutes, it is therefore better to do this with the pans partially offset on the Boiling Plate as this hotplate will recuperate the fastest after use. At other times, however, you may prefer to transfer vegetables to the Simmering Plate for a few minutes' boiling before draining and transferring to the Simmering Oven to finish cooking.

Foods Requiring High Temperatures Always ensure that foods requiring the very highest temperatures are cooked when the cooker is at its fullest heat storage. In practice this is easy to do and fits in with normal routines. Plan to bake bread first thing after breakfast or after a period where little cooking has taken place. Yorkshire puddings (*see* page 132) can be cooked early in the day before everything else for the very best rise – they re-heat beautifully in the Roasting Oven just before serving. Similarly, when making jam and marmalade, it is best to do this before cooking a lot of other food. Add sugar which has been warmed in the Simmering Oven to cooked fruit on the Simmering Plate. When the sugar is fully dissolved, transfer to the Boiling Plate where the full reserve of heat immediately brings a rapid rolling boil, producing preserves with exceptionally bright colours. So when the very fastest response is required on the hotplate, always bring things to temperature elsewhere first and then transfer to the Boiling Plate for the required length of time and you will enjoy sustained high temperature cooking. The same principle applies when using the Aga wok. Pre-heat it first until it is good and hot before placing it on the Boiling Plate and starting to cook.

Correct Utensils Essential Aga utensils are designed for maximum efficiency. The utensils you use must have very thick and absolutely flat bases to ensure perfect contact with the Aga hotplates. In this way, you will never need to have the insulated lids up for prolonged periods and will therefore retain the valuable stores of heat. A pan that is slow to come to the boil wastes the stored heat. By using saucepans with stacking lids such as found with Aga utensils, you are able to cook with as many as seven pans in the Simmering Oven at one time.

5. THE 7 MINUTE PRINCIPLE

Everything that takes place on the hotplates should typically take no more than 7 minutes. On the Boiling Plate these processes are usually extremely rapid: bringing things quickly to the boil, searing in the grill pan, sizzling fast stir-frying, toasting and deep fat frying. On the Simmering Plate the transfer of heat is slower, but again taking little more than 7 minutes: heating milk, making sauces, toasted sandwiches, etc. If you are therefore cooking something on the top of the cooker for much longer, it is a good idea to ask yourself, 'Could I, or should I, be cooking this better somewhere else in the cooker?' The answer in most cases will be one of the oven scenarios already discussed in the 80:20 Principle section. To help you easily get into the habit of making the most use of the Aga ovens, keep this question in mind every time you start to cook something on the top of the cooker.

Cooking in the oven means no mess to clean up and food will hardly require any supervision.

Of course, there a few exceptions which take longer, where constant supervision is essential, such as when boiling jam for a set. If something needs your close inspection then it should have exactly that: cook whatever it is on the top to make sure it is cooked just how you want. Otherwise, keep times short on the top and move the food somewhere else within the cooker as soon as possible. If you use the hotplates like this, you never need to be afraid to lift the lids and use the hotplates when you need them – there will then always be plenty of stored heat for all cooking operations. In this way you will fall quickly into good Aga discipline and find that your lids miraculously spend most of their time as they should do: down! You will also realise the immediate benefits of experiencing minimal heat loss and possessing a very clean Aga. Keep at the back of your mind the simple command, 'Think Oven!' and you will discover a life of no fuss, no mess, no smells, just simply good cooking.

6. THE START AND TRANSFER PRINCIPLE

Starting something off in a hot part of the cooker and then transferring it to finish cooking in another part of the cooker is a guiding philosophy for getting the best out of your Aga. Start something off to get it 'on its way' and then transfer elsewhere in the cooker to finish cooking. On the top of the Aga the Boiling Plate is used most often to start things off. If, however, you were re-heating a thickened sauce or casserole, this would start to splash as it was heated, and the Simmering Plate would in this case be a better choice. Keep the pan covered and stir occasionally until it is gently simmering, then transfer to the Simmering Oven.

Almost without exception, foods cooked in the Simmering Oven are heated first elsewhere, either on, or in the cooker. Many things can be started off in the Roasting Oven, but to get utensils as hot as possible before use, they must be placed on the Boiling Plate to come to their full heat before being used.

Here is a selection of common examples to get you started. They are all easy to apply both to everyday cooking and when entertaining. You will soon think of others once you understand the basic principle.

Start to heat onions and garlic on the Boiling Plate for just a minute, before **transferring** to the Simmering Oven to soften and become tender in the early stages of making soups, stews and casseroles (*see* page 30).

Start potatoes and root vegetables off with 3-5 minutes' boiling on the Boiling Plate or Simmering Plate, before draining and **transferring** to the Simmering Oven to steam (*see* page 31).

Start to heat an Aga wok on the Simmering Plate until very hot, before **transferring** to the Boiling Plate to heat to a very high temperature for a stir-fry (*see* page 63).

Start rice and pasta off with a minute's boiling on the Boiling Plate, before **transferring**, covered, to the Simmering Oven (*see* page 31).

Start to grill in the pre-heated cast-iron grill pan on the Boiling Plate, before **transferring** the pan to the floor of the Roasting Oven (*see* page 26).

Start milk puddings in the Roasting Oven, before **transferring** to the Simmering Oven for several hours to finish cooking (*see* page 32).

Start a roast off in the Roasting Oven, before **transferring** to the Baking or Simmering Oven for medium or slow roasting techniques (*see* pages 26-27).

Start a fruit pie on the floor of the Roasting Oven until the pastry is perfectly cooked, before **transferring** to the Simmering Oven to finish cooking the filling (*see* page 31).

Start a steamed pudding off with 30 minutes' boiling on the Simmering Plate, before **transferring** to the Simmering Oven to finish steaming (*see* page 31).

Start a cake requiring a moderate baking temperature in the Roasting Oven with a cold plain shelf above, before **transferring** to the Simmering Oven to finish cooking (*see* page 31).

Start a gratin at the very top of the Roasting Oven to brown it, before **transferring** to a lower oven position to allow the potatoes to become tender (*see* page 26).

Start a crumble in the Roasting Oven until the topping is golden, before **transferring** to the Simmering Oven to finish cooking the fruit (*see* page 31).

Start a turkey in the Roasting Oven to begin its cooking, before **transferring** to a cooler oven for medium or slow roasting (*see* pages 32-33).

Start a layered pasta dish such as lasagne low down in the Roasting Oven to get it thoroughly hot and cooked, before **transferring** to the very top of the Roasting Oven if necessary, to finish browning before serving (*see* page 26).

Start a sauce on the Simmering Plate, before **transferring** to the Simmering or Warming Oven to finish cooking or keep hot (*see* pages 32 and 35).

Start to heat oil in a deep fish fryer on the Simmering Plate until hot, before **transferring** to the Boiling Plate for heating to a high temperature (*see* pages 9-11).

7. THE SHIELDING PRINCIPLE

This is an important principle to understand. As we have seen, because the ovens are heated by radiant heat, and not circulating hot air, the ovens cook by heat zones that can be shielded by using a deflecting plate. The heat is in fact invisible infra-red light that converts to heat when absorbed by food. It is radiated from all the surfaces of the oven onto the food and this is the main reason for the wonderful results the Aga produces. The strongest radiation of heat comes from right at the top of the Roasting Oven. This is why when you want to grill for or brown something quickly, it should be placed high up so that it is almost touching the roof of the oven. The cold plain shelf supplied with every new Aga is designed for two purposes. In both cases it should start off cold and it should never be stored in the ovens. The first and obvious use is for cooking scones, rolls and biscuits, etc. However its main purpose is to create a more moderate baking temperature in the Roasting Oven when this is required. This is particularly important when baking cakes with the 2 oven Aga, as the Roasting Oven on this model also doubles as a Baking Oven. A cold plain shelf is inserted above certain foods to shield them and give protection from the strong browning from the top of the oven. It does *not* cool down the oven as some owners suppose. It merely provides a physical barrier which deflects the heat from above to cause the zone below it to become more moderate for a short period of 20-30 minutes. After this time it will lose its effect. Replacing it with a fresh cold plain shelf will extend the period of protection. A full size Aga baking tray or roasting tin may also be used in this way. Food requiring a high temperature can of course be cooked at the same time at the top of the oven, or even on the cold plain shelf itself.

The 'Home' position for the cold plain shelf, mainly when baking in a 2 oven Aga, is on the second set of runners from the top. However, the lower it is inserted, the greater the shielding effect. For most recipes the Home position should be used by inserting the cold plain shelf at the same time as the cake is added to the oven below. Usually the cake needs to be set on the grid shelf on the floor of the oven, or the lowest set of runners. A very few recipes require the cold plain shelf to be positioned lower and this can be used if a very moderate oven is required, for example when baking a large deep sponge cake. *See* the Aga Baking Conversion Matrix, beginning on page 88, for complete Aga baking instructions.

There are other uses for the shielding principle which can be used on all models of cooker. Here are some examples to give you an idea of what happens under certain conditions:

Situation You are cooking an assembled layered dish such as lasagne or moussaka, made the day before, as an easy supper dish. It has cooked in the suggested position in the Roasting Oven, probably on the grid shelf on the floor of the oven or possibly on the lowest set of runners, for about 30-35 minutes. You check it after 30 minutes and it is perfectly browned. However, as you have cooked it from the refrigerator you want to make sure it is piping hot and cooked in the middle but don't want it to brown any further.

Solution *Simply slide in the cold plain shelf above and it will continue to heat through and bake to the centre without browning much more because of the shielding principle.*

Situation You are cooking a large number of baked potatoes for a party. You place two trays full of potatoes in the oven, one on the lowest set of runners and another on the second set of runners. You bake for the normal time you are used to for cooking one tray of potatoes. When you go to test them, you find that the lower tray are only half cooked.

Solution *Swap the trays around half way through cooking. The upper tray of potatoes has acted like a cold plain shelf – instead of a metal shelf you have used a thick potato layer which is quite dense. Cooking a large quantity of food on any cooker usually takes longer than preparing normal quantities.* See *pages 119-127 for advice on cooking for large numbers.*

Situation You are cooking a traybake which normally requires a cold plain shelf above when baking in the Roasting Oven in a 2 oven Aga. However, you are also grilling four gammon steaks at the top of the oven.

Solution *As the gammon steaks are in an Aga baking tray, this will act as a cold plain shelf without a separate one being required.*

Situation You are cooking some roast potatoes. You allow an hour and a half but since they are a different variety to your usual potato, they cook and brown a little more quickly than expected. They are perfect and you don't want them to cook much more. You want to keep them hot and crisp while the rest of the meal finishes cooking but transferring them to the Simmering Oven would tend to make them go soggy.

Solution *Transfer the cooked potatoes to an oven-proof serving dish and place in the coolest part of the Roasting or Baking Oven, which is on a grid shelf or an Aga toaster on the floor of the oven. To keep them hot for 20-30 minutes without further browning, slide in a cold plain shelf just above them.*

Situation You are baking some biscuits in a 2 oven Aga after a busy morning cooking for the weekend. Normally these are baked low down in the oven with a cold plain shelf above on the second set of runners, and you follow the usual method for your first batch, using a cold plain shelf above. When you check the biscuits after their full cooking time of 10 minutes, you discover that they are only half cooked.

Solution *Allow a further three to five minutes until they are cooked. Obviously, as you have done quite a lot of cooking during the morning, the oven is a little cooler than usual. So, when you bake your second batch you remove the hot plain shelf as you know that the biscuits will cook happily for the normal time low down without needing a plain shelf for protection.*

THE AMAZING CAPACITY OF AN AGA

Glance through a magazine, and you could be forgiven for thinking that double ovens, slow cookers and ovens that help to clean themselves are the very latest developments in cooker technology. The truth is, they're all features that have been enjoyed by Aga owners for the last seventy-five years. But typically, the Aga cooker adopted all three principles and many more in its own inimitable but very practical fashion.

The dimensions of all the ovens are approximately the same. Because the ovens are indirectly heated, every square inch of the ovens can be used. They can all be packed with a large amount of food when necessary. Conventional ovens require room to be left for hot air to circulate. It is for this reason that each of the ovens can accommodate a 28 lb (13kg) turkey, the Roasting Oven being able to fast roast one of this size to absolute perfection in as little as 4 hours. The oven will also accommodate a 22lb (9kg) roast of beef or four legs of lamb. When cooking a lot of food, as with any oven, allow a little longer composite cooking time, as a large mass of cold food takes longer to cook.

The size of Aga ovens is deceptive, they appear to be quite small as the doors are smaller than on conventional cookers, but the depth ensures that several roasting tins can be placed in one oven at a time. For example, in the Roasting Oven you could, if you wished, simultaneously cook a tray of roast potatoes, a 4 lb (1.82kg) roast chicken, bake an apple pie, cook 8 baked potatoes, 8 vol-au-vent cases and start off a 2 pint (1.2l) rice pudding. Because the ovens are vented, there is no confusion of flavours between sweet and savoury dishes. This means that you can, if you wish, bake a Victoria Sandwich with some kippers and garlic bread all at the same time in the same oven!

As well as understanding the capacity of the Roasting Oven, the Simmering Oven is equally capacious and this means that you can fit up to seven Aga pans at one time. You can, for example, cook the following simultaneously in the Simmering Oven:

Boston Baked Beans, French Onion Soup, Sticky Toffee Pudding, 2 pints (1.2l) Béchamel Sauce, 2 pints (1.2l) Custard, New Potatoes with Mint and Steamed Glazed Carrots.

I hope that I've whetted your appetite to explore the tremendous capacity of your Aga.

THE AGA OVENS

THE HEAT INDICATOR

It is important that you run your Aga with the mercury of the heat indicator on or just above the black line within the central silver section (*see right*). For the first few days after it is installed this should be checked and the thermostat very slightly advanced or retarded to achieve this. Once this correct setting has been determined, no further regulation is necessary or recommended. You simply don't need to, and shouldn't, touch the control again apart from switching the cooker off. Temperature is automatically controlled which liberates the cook to concentrate on the actual cooking in hand.

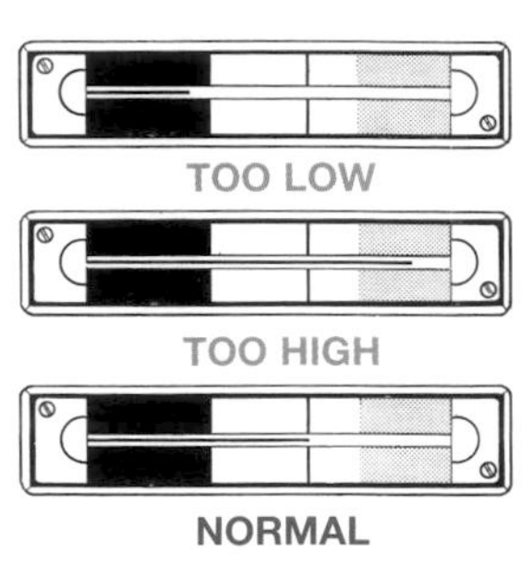

OVEN TEMPERATURES YOU CAN TRUST

One of the most common questions new Aga owners ask, quite naturally, is, 'What exactly are the temperatures of the Aga ovens?' There is no need to test the ovens with thermometers – the centre air temperatures are in fact rather misleading if you try and compare them with ones in conventional recipes. Temperatures are not directly comparable and in fact become less important. Simply remember that all cooking in the Aga is conducted according to positioning and timing. By following the Aga method and oven positions recommended, you will find where your favourite recipes cook best. Use the 'What Cooks Where' section that follows as a general guide. If you have an older Aga you may find that the Simmering Oven is cooler than a modern Aga and cooking times will therefore need to be longer. If an Aga is reconditioned or converted in fuel type, heat distribution within the cooker may be different, and oven temperatures will often be at considerable variance to those found in a new Aga, especially with the Simmering Oven.

Follow the Aga method and positionings and you will always get excellent results. There is also quite a bit of flexibility, if you cook something a little higher or lower than the suggested position, the food will just cook and brown a little more quickly or slowly. If you are cooking a lot of food at the same time, sometimes things that normally are cooked in a certain position can be moved slightly so that everything can cook at the same time. As with any cooker, all timings given are approximate, and there is never a problem to take a look and see how things are progressing. In this way you will instinctively get a feel for appropriate timings. Oven runners are counted from the top of the oven downwards.

Aga oven	Temperature	Celsius	Fahrenheit	British Gas Mark
Roasting Oven	Hot	Approx. 240-260°C	475-500°F	Gas Mark 8-9
Baking Oven	Moderate	Approx. 180-200°C	350-400°F	Gas Mark 4-6
Simmering Oven	Slow	Approx. 115-135°C	225-275°F	Gas Mark 1
Warming Oven	Warm	Approx. 70-90°C	150-200°F	Gas Mark 1/4

A chart for the die-hard 'I simply must know the temperature' owners, who want to be sure that their Aga cookers are operating correctly. Please bear in mind the explanation above.

THE AGA OVENS: WHAT COOKS WHERE

OVEN DYNAMICS

Here is a breakdown of the cooking conditions within each oven, showing where different foods should be cooked. Positionings are graduated from right at the very top, down the sets of runners, to using the actual floor of the oven for cooking some foods. Read this section in conjunction with the diagram of your Aga at the very back of the book.

ROASTING OVEN

SIMMERING OVEN

BAKING OVEN

WARMING OVEN

This oven is always hot and immediately ready for cooking food extremely fast. It is very large and evenly heated throughout, with the left-hand side and back, nearest the heat source, being very slightly hotter. Every cubic inch of space in the oven can be used. This constant radiation of heat all round ensures even cooking and the controlled heat gives you complete freedom from burning. It is even unnecessary to baste a joint, and it will hardly shrink at all – this is because the radiant heat seals in all the juices, and of course all of the flavour. Because of the 'kind-to-food' heat you will find that you don't have to watch over food so much to prevent it becoming dried out or burnt. The cast iron ovens are also humidity controlled, with correct ventilation and a simple vent to carry steam and cooking smells away to the outside. On models with a conventional flue or powerflue this is automatic. On other models a manual control is used to turn a fan on to provide this venting. This oven venting system means that in effect you have a built-in cooker extraction canopy and a conventional cooker hood is simply not needed. The oven vent is situated at the back of the ovens, so always place foods towards the back of the oven when possible so steam and cooking smells are removed more efficiently. This also helps to keep the door lining from getting splashed.

ROASTING OVEN: OVEN GRILLING

For grilling, place the food on a grill rack in the high position in an Aga roasting tin and hang at the top of the oven on the highest set of runners. Sausages and bacon cook beautifully here (*see* pages 57-61 for breakfast ideas). Also meat patties and thick pork chops cook well here. Flat fish also grill well after being brushed with a little melted butter. For browning gratins, layered potato and potato-topped dishes such as fish pie, shepherd's pie and cottage pie, cook in the middle of the oven. Before serving, brush with a little salted milk or melted butter if necessary, then place on a grid shelf as high as you can, with the surface to be browned almost touching the roof of the oven to get the potato perfectly browned.

ROASTING OVEN: FAST ROASTING

Roast meat by the fast method here using the same traditional times as with any other cooker with the Aga roasting tin hanging from the lowest set of runners. As a guide, for beef: allow 15 minutes per lb (450g) and 15 minutes over; for lamb, 20 minutes per lb (450g) and 20 minutes over. Allow a little less if you like your meat rare: for beef, 12 minutes per lb (450g) and 12 minutes over; for lamb, 15 minutes per lb (450g) and 15 minutes over. For pork, allow 30 minutes per lb (450g) and 30 minutes over; for veal 20 minutes per lb (450g) and 20 minutes over. For chicken, allow about 45 minutes for 2 lb (900g), 1-1¼ hours for 3 lb (1.5kg), 1½ hours for 4 lb (1.75kg) and 1¾ hours for 5 lb (2.25kg) birds. For duck, allow about 1 – 1½ hours, depending on size and how you like your duck. For pheasant and partridge, allow about 45-60 minutes for one to four birds. For grouse allow 20-30 minutes and for woodcock, snipe or quail allow about 12-15 minutes. For roast turkey and goose and boned and rolled poultry roasts, *see* pages 111-119, within the Christmas section.

PERFECT OPEN ROASTING

Use an Aga grill rack set in the low position if liked when roasting. I recommend the use of an inexpensive meat thermometer for roasting meat and poultry by all methods. It is then possible to ensure that meat and poultry are safely roasted so that the two extremes of under and over cooking are avoided. A dial type meat thermometer left in a roast whilst cooking is inexpensive or alternatively a digital probe may be used. I also prefer to roast with a few onions and root vegetables in the tin which roast and brown to help ensure a rich colour and flavour when making gravy. For poultry I like to stuff the cavity of the bird with onion, lemon, herbs, etc., and smear the breast with a little softened butter and cover with some streaky bacon.

PERFECT ROAST VEGETABLES

Roast potatoes and other vegetables cook best with the roasting tin directly on the floor of the oven, where the punch of heat from below gives just the conditions needed. If you are cooking several trays, place these elsewhere in this oven, but swap the trays around periodically to ensure they all enjoy a good spell of crisping on the floor. Goose fat makes the best roast potatoes and parsnips, if this is not available, a mixture of half vegetable shortening and half olive oil works brilliantly.

ROASTING OVEN: BAKING

High temperature baking is best undertaken in the Roasting Oven. Strong and consistent heat is perfect for cooking scones and pastries. Generally the second and third set of runners are best for cooking scones and puff pastry items. The third set of runners give Yorkshire puddings (*see* page 132) the highest heat whilst allowing sufficient space for the batter to expand spectacularly.

2 oven Aga Baking Moderate Baking may be undertaken in a 2 oven Aga by positioning foods in the coolest part of the Roasting Oven. Place on a grid shelf on the floor of the oven and insert a cold plain shelf above on the second set of runners. Tray bakes, Victoria Sandwiches, muffins and biscuits etc. use this technique. The cold plain shelf can shield food from the aggressive browning above for 20-30 minutes as long as it is inserted cold. 3 and 4 oven Aga owners should use the Baking Oven instead for these foods and generally, no plain shelf will be required.

Very Moderate Baking may be undertaken in a 2 oven Aga by positioning foods in the coolest part of the Roasting Oven. Place on a grid shelf on the floor of the oven and insert a cold plain shelf above on the second set of runners. After 20-25 minutes, replace the cold shelf with another cold plain shelf, Aga baking tray or full size roasting tin. For some recipes the food can then be transferred to the Simmering Oven to finish cooking, in some cases onto the transferred hot plain shelf from the Roasting Oven.

The Baking Oven should be used on other models for medium temperature baking, with a cold plain shelf above being very occasionally necessary. Fruit crumbles are one example where different methods of cooking can be used, depending on your model: protected in the Roasting Oven with a cold plain shelf above and then transferred to the Simmering Oven in a 2 oven cooker. In 3 and 4 oven cookers they may be cooked for the whole time on the third set of runners in the Baking Oven.

For large deep cakes, the Aga Cake Baker may be used in the 2 oven Aga. For a comprehensive aide-mémoire, use the Aga Baking Conversion Matrix, beginning on page 90.

Baked potatoes cook best on the third set of runners. Prick with a fork and rub a little oil over the skin to speed cooking and give a good crunch.

Poach fish on the lowest set of runners. There is no need for special equipment such as an expensive fish kettle. Remove the head or if necessary, cut the fish in half to fit the tin. Season the cavity well and add some aromatics. Wrap in buttered foil and then a second layer of wide foil. Place diagonally in a full size roasting tin or in two packages next to each other. Pour boiling water to come just half-way up the tin. Slide carefully onto the lowest set of runners. Allow 5 minutes per lb (450g), slightly less for more than 8 lb (3.6kg). Turn fish over half-way through cooking. Remove from the oven, leave until warm and then skin. If serving hot allow 25% extra cooking time.

Bake fish in an ovenproof container on a grid shelf on the floor of the Roasting Oven.

ROASTING OVEN: OVEN FRYING

The floor of the Roasting Oven is a 'hidden hotplate': it is a large extension to the Boiling and Simmering Plates. It is approximately of a temperature somewhere between the two hotplates. Use it for great results and you will discover that no mess is created and the top of the cooker is left free for other things. Instead of frying sausages on the top of the cooker and making a mess, fry in a cast-iron pan or in a roasting tin on the floor of the Roasting Oven. It will only take a couple of shakes of the utensil during cooking to turn the sausages and achieve even browning. Frying in a container on the floor of the oven is very easy and keeps mess to a minimum. Food also tends to require less turning and supervision. Breakfast frying is done to perfection – place the bacon, sausages, tomatoes, etc., in an Aga roasting tin and stand it directly on the floor of the oven. Once everything else is almost cooked, even eggs can be added to the tin and returned to the floor of the oven to cook beautifully. For exceptionally crisp American-style bacon, fry on Bake-O-Glide on a baking tray on the floor of the oven without any further fat.

Battered or breadcrumbed fish can be shallow fried in a little vegetable or sunflower oil in an Aga roasting tin. Pre-heat the oil for a few minutes until just starting to smoke, then cook placing the presentation side down first.

To fry onions until golden, start in a pan on the Simmering Plate and then transfer to the floor of the oven to colour gradually to just the shade you require. Carefully browning onions for French Onion Soup is greatly simplified using this method. If making a large casserole, floured pieces of meat can even be browned in batches here, but do not over-crowd the container.

ROASTING OVEN: BREAD, PASTRY AND PIZZAS

The Roasting Oven is the nearest thing to a traditional brick baker's oven or of the type found in authentic pizzerias. Loaves of bread bake best on a grid shelf on the floor of the oven. For rolls, bake on a baking sheet on the third or fourth set of runners. If making a rustic loaf or soda bread, cook these directly on the floor of the oven. Use an Aga Baker's Paddle or slide the loaf in sitting on a piece of Bake-O-Glide.

If baking a tart or double crust pie start on the floor of the oven to ensure that the bottom crust is thoroughly cooked before raising the pie later to finish browning the top if necessary

There is no need to bake blind when cooking a quiche, flan or pastry case. For quiches and flans, add your sweet or savoury custard just before baking and cook on the floor of the oven.
The pastry will cook quickly and crisply and the filling will set and brown without making the base at all soggy.

If an empty pastry case is required, e.g. for a lemon meringue pie, gypsy tart or banoffi pie roll out and prick the pastry and place in the freezer for several hours. Bake from frozen on the floor of the oven and no beans or paper will be required.

Home-made and bought pizzas cook to perfection directly on the floor of the oven – two will fit in at the same time. If you need to cook more, transfer the first two to the top of the oven to brown the topping while you start the next two on the floor. Allow about 8-10 minutes cooking time.

SIMMERING OVEN

The Simmering Oven is a 'continuation' oven, i.e. generally anything cooked there will continue to cook if it has already been heated up first. Depending on the density and thermal inertia of food, an appropriate length of time should be allowed for sufficient thermal momentum to develop. Apart from large masses of solid foods, as a guide allow about 5 minutes once something has been brought to temperature elsewhere on or in the cooker, before transferring to this oven. Fish and cheesecakes finish cooking here after being started in the Roasting Oven. Wonderfully creamy milk puddings, baked custards and steamed puddings of all sorts are cooked slowly and gently without any further attention. Pâtés and terrine dishes finish cooking here for 2-3 hours after 30 minutes' cooking in a water bath in the Roasting Oven with a cold plain shelf above. Pulses can also be slowly rendered tender after an initial 30 minutes on the Simmering Plate.

SIMMERING OVEN: CASSEROLES, STEWS AND SOUPS

For casseroles, stews and soups, use your favourite recipes, browning meat if you wish, followed by other ingredients in a non-stick frying pan, and then assembling in a casserole or sauté in batches in the casserole itself. Add your chosen liquids and flavourings and then transfer to the Simmering Plate and bring to a very gentle simmer for a few minutes. Cover and transfer to the floor of the Simmering Oven for normal slow cooking times, $1\frac{1}{2}$-3 hours, or on a grid shelf or Aga toaster on the floor for ultra slow cooking, 3-5 hours.

SIMMERING OVEN: STEAMING VEGETABLES, RICE AND FISH; COOKING PASTA AND COUSCOUS; BOILING AND STEAMING BACON AND GAMMON

Potatoes and all types of root vegetable can be most successfully cooked in the Aga by using the Simmering Oven to steam them until they are perfectly tender. The technique locks in all the flavour and goodness. Cut into even-sized pieces, just cover with cold salted water and bring to the boil on the Boiling Plate. Adjust the pan on the Boiling Plate or transfer to the Simmering Plate and slow boil for 3-5 minutes. Drain off all the water (saving the water for gravies and soups), cover and transfer to the Simmering Oven for 20-40 minutes, depending on variety and the size you have cut the pieces. Old potatoes, which would normally turn to mush with ordinary boiling, remain whole and floury and new potatoes steamed with mint are a revelation.

Rice is easily cooked by the absorption method. Measure the rice by volume, I use a mug for two adult portions. Now use the same measure to give twice the volume of water or stock. Add a little salt and bring to the boil. Cover and transfer to the Simmering Oven for 20-30 minutes. Simple pilau rice recipes can be easily adapted to use this technique which guarantees perfect results every time, with every grain fluffy and separate.

Pasta should be brought to the boil in a large pan of salted water, covered and then transferred to the Simmering Oven for the time directed on the packet. No oil need be added to the water and the pasta will not stick.

Couscous can be cooked by adding boiling water (allow 1 pint (600ml) per 9 oz (250g). Cover and transfer to the Simmering Oven for 5-10 minutes to absorb the water and keep hot. Uncover and fork through before adding butter or other ingredients.

Fish steams perfectly in a container with just a little hot liquid in this oven. Pack into an oven-proof dish and add a little fish stock or half and half water and milk. Cook on the floor of the Roasting Oven for 5 minutes and then transfer to finish cooking in the Simmering Oven for 12-20 minutes, until just cooked.

Bacon and gammon joints can be boiled or steamed. After an all-important overnight soak in lots of cold water, drain and place on an enamelled plate in a large pan. To boil, just cover with fresh water. To steam, pour in 2-3 inches (5-7cm) of cold water. Bring slowly to the boil and then cover and simmer for 20-30 minutes on the Simmering Plate. Transfer to the Simmering Oven, allowing a total cooking time of approximately 25 minutes per lb (450g).

SIMMERING OVEN: SLOW ROASTING

Calculate your total cooking time for normal fast roasting and then start off with the roasting tin hanging on the lowest set of runners in the Roasting Oven. Allow 30 minutes for the roast to start to brown, 45 minutes for roasts more than 8 lbs (3.6kg). For turkey timings, *see* pages 115-116 of the Christmas section. Then transfer to the Simmering Oven for double the remaining cooking time. Return to the Roasting Oven to crisp if necessary before the final resting.

SIMMERING OVEN: KEEPING FOOD HOT, WARMING PLATES, OFF-PEAK AND OVERNIGHT COOKERY

The Simmering Oven is perfect for keeping cooked food hot and for warming plates in 2 and 3 oven cookers. If food requires no further cooking, avoid placing it in direct contact with the floor of the oven or near the top as both these positions will be slightly hotter than elsewhere. Therefore place on a grid shelf instead in this oven. Stock, whether simple everyday stock from a leftover chicken or from raw beef, poultry or veal bones, is simple to make leaving the pan on a grid shelf on the floor of the oven for many hours or overnight.
Aga Porridge made with oatmeal cooks gently overnight in a tightly covered pan on a grid shelf on the floor of this oven. Christmas puddings can also finish steaming overnight. When making sauces such as Béchamel, heat the milk here in a Pyrex jug for 30 minutes beforehand to speed up the process. Cooked sauces can be prepared ahead and kept hot in covered pans or jugs covered with clingfilm until wanted. To prevent skins forming, float pieces of wetted baking parchment onto the surfaces or in the case of milk sauces, pour over a little cold milk to be whisked in at the last minute. Add final flavourings, herbs or cheese just before using.

SIMMERING OVEN: THE EXCEPTIONS AND FOODS STARTED FROM COLD

Rich and deliciously moist fruitcakes can cook over several hours here and you can produce meringues that are the envy of experts in just a couple of hours. Sugar for jam making can be warmed and jars sterilised. The whole of the oven can be used for drying herbs, fruits and mushrooms, etc. – the list goes on and on. Some of life's little luxuries such as delicious lemon curd can even be made in the jar without using a double saucepan or needing to stir, as can fudge, candied peel and marrons glacés (*see* page 130).

ROASTING OVEN

SIMMERING OVEN

BAKING OVEN

WARMING OVEN

3 and 4 oven Aga Cookers feature a Baking Oven which is a dedicated moderate baking oven – high temperature baking is always conducted in the Roasting Oven. It is the perfect temperature for pastries and cakes. Many foods cooked in the Roasting Oven can also be cooked in the Baking Oven, but for a longer time.

BAKING OVEN: FAST ROASTING

The Baking Oven may be used for the fast roasting method described under the Roasting Oven section after the roast has been started off in the Roasting Oven. This is suitable for all joints of meat and poultry with the exception of turkeys and geese (*see* separate timings on pages 115-116 of the Christmas section). Start the roast off for 30-45 minutes in the Roasting Oven, depending on size, and then transfer to the Baking Oven to finish fast roasting. Place the roasting tin as high in the oven as possible. The joint will cook in virtually the same time as using the Roasting Oven and the advantage of this method is that the Roasting Oven is then left free for cooking Yorkshire puddings (*see* page 132), roast vegetables and trimmings.

BAKING OVEN: MODERATE ROASTING

All joints of meat and poultry, with the exception of turkeys and geese, may be roasted from scratch in the Baking Oven, allowing 30%-40% longer than that required for the normal fast roasting method. Turkeys and geese may be roasted with the moderate roasting method but it is essential that these are given a preliminary period in the Roasting Oven. *See* separate timings on pages 115-116 of the Christmas section.

BAKING OVEN: MODERATE BAKING

The Baking Oven is, correctly speaking, a moderate baking oven, and is perfect for many types of baking which do not require the higher temperature of the Roasting Oven. Small cakes are cooked at the top of the oven and the second or third set of runners down are suitable for tray bakes, chocolate brownies, muffins and fruit crumbles. Biscuits cook better on the lowest sets of runners and Victoria Sandwiches and shortbreads on a grid shelf on the floor of the oven.

Auxiliary Bread Baking: if a large amount of bread is already being baked in the Roasting Oven, further loaves may also be baked in this oven, but the tins should be placed directly on the oven floor to speed the baking.

BAKING OVEN: BAKING, STEAMING AND POACHING FISH; BAKING SOUFFLES AND CHEESECAKES

Fish steams perfectly in a container with just a little liquid in the middle of this oven. Fish may also be baked with no added water in the same position. To poach fish including kippers and smoked haddock, just pour over a little boiling water in an Aga roasting tin, and leave on the floor of this oven for 5-8 minutes until just cooked. Soufflés rise steadily on the fourth set of runners with no danger of falling if the door is opened to check. Cheesecakes bake well on a grid shelf on the floor of the oven.

BAKING OVEN: THICKENING SAUCES, FUDGE AND CHUTNEY

With a grid shelf placed on the floor of this oven, pans which have started to cook food at a moderate rate may be placed here to continue cooking. They will require no further attention for up to 10 minutes with no fear of mixtures 'catching'. Examples include cooking out the flour in a Béchamel or other white sauce once the hot milk has been incorporated, if a longer time in the Simmering Oven is not possible. Fudge mixtures may continue to boil once they register the correct temperature. Similarly, chutneys and relishes may be left here for even longer and reduced until the final stage needs to be undertaken with supervision. Because this oven is vented the mixture will continue to reduce. Do not leave pans for more than 30 minutes using this last technique.

WARMING OVEN

This part of the Aga is perfect for entertaining. Cooked food can be kept hot for hours without drying out, cooking further or deteriorating. Though the temperature is quite sufficient, it will not crack or craze the most delicate china. Place plates and serving dishes here in plenty of time to warm through thoroughly before they are wanted. Cooked food that requires no further cooking can be kept hot here either in pans with tight-fitting lids or in tureens covered temporarily with dinner plates. Warm tureen lids and gravy boats on the Warming Plate so that they are heated but the handles are still cool enough to hold. This maximises the amount that can be stowed away in this oven. Plated meals can also be stacked to keep food hot for latecomers. Cooked sauces can be prepared ahead and kept hot in covered pans or jugs covered with cling film until wanted. To prevent skins forming, float pieces of wetted baking parchment onto the surfaces or in the case of milk sauces, pour over a little cold milk to be whisked in at the last minute. Add final flavourings, herbs or cheese just before using. Cooked joints may be rested in this oven as an alternative to using the Warming Plate. Meringues may also be made in this oven as well as in the Simmering Oven.

DIVIDING OVENS: MAXIMISING YOUR COOKER'S VERSATILITY

Under certain circumstances it can be an advantage to use a plain shelf to divide an oven temporarily. The lower right cast iron Simmering Oven found on 2 and 3 oven cookers only, can be usefully divided into two compartments with a plain shelf if desired. This can be useful when cooking a lot of food such as for a roast meal. This oven can also serve the purpose of the Simmering and Warming Ovens found on the 4 oven Aga with two distinct temperature zones. Place the shelf in the middle of the oven for several hours. After some time the top half will be slightly hotter, perfect for steaming potatoes and root vegetables as well food requiring slow cooking. The lower section will be cooler and ideal for warming plates and serving dishes and for keeping cooked food hot without spoiling. Where the Simmering Oven is divided using the single runners on a 4 oven model, the temperature remains constant throughout.

A cold plain shelf added to a Roasting or Baking Oven, and left for at least 40 minutes, will to a certain extent have the effect of concentrating the heat in the top part of the oven. Some owners use this principle when they encounter a forgotten shelf and take the opportunity to cook foods such as Yorkshire puddings (*see* page 132). Under normal circumstances there is no need for this resort; excellent Yorkshire puddings may be made using the top half of the Roasting Oven at normal temperature for immediate use, or for preparing ahead of time and then re-heating.

2. AGA 'BATTERIE DE CUISINE'

Choosing cookware, I always feel, is a very personal issue. Aga do not insist that you use their cookware, but I know from experience that you will get better results if you do. In recent years the Aga Cook Shop Collection has expanded hugely, and there is now tremendous choice, so that you can build up the perfect collection of Aga cookware to suit your cooking and your family's needs. All the items in the range are designed to give years of service and it is fun to build up gradually your own personal collection.

I am often asked for advice on which cookware is best and I feel that it is a very subjective matter. For a start, there are so many different materials to consider – cast-iron, stainless steel, hard anodised aluminium as well as cast aluminium. All have their uses – different products are popular for various reasons with different people. I have moved over largely to using a lot more stainless steel in recent years for the simple reason that it can all go in the dishwasher. To some people, that in itself is not an issue; they insist that washing pans by machine takes up too much valuable space in the dishwasher. People who wash up by hand often prefer aluminium. I certainly use some hard anodised aluminium pans for a number of purposes and I am also a huge fan of my two cast aluminium pans which get pressed into service for a lot of other jobs. The cast-iron range is also perfect for oven-to-tableware with its smart enamel finish.

In this section, I share with you why, because of its design, Aga cookware performs better, and guide you through my personal favourites – from my recommended 'must-have' items to helping you to compile your own 'would-like-to-have' list. My recommendations are also based on grass roots feedback from many thousands of Aga owners over the years at demonstrations, workshops, exhibitions and food fairs.

COOKWARE POINTERS

CORRECT BASES ESSENTIAL

The perfectly flat surfaces of the cast iron Aga hotplates are actually machined to a tolerance of 0.25mm to give a dead flat surface. Heat is only efficiently transferred by conduction to utensils when direct contact is made with the surface of a hotplate. If utensils with a poor base are used, only a few points on the base will receive heat. This results in uneven heating, causing slow boiling and making control difficult which can cause food to burn. Inefficient utensils also mean that the insulating lids need to be up for long periods and this, of course, is a waste of the cooker's stored heat.

Therefore, to get the best results from the Aga hotplates, it is important to use utensils that have thick and perfectly flat bases so that they make good contact. After much careful trial and experimentation, I have come to the conclusion that the Aga range of utensils really is the best and I recommend using these. Due to the construction and finish of their bases, they give far superior results and no other range currently available works as efficiently. There are two important reasons for this. Firstly, Aga utensils have 6mm ($^{1}/_{4}$ inch) thick bases so that over many years of use on the hot Aga Boiling Plate they will not warp or distort. Secondly, the bases are not just thick, they are also precision finished to make the all-important direct contact across the whole of their bases for the most efficient transfer of heat. This enables you to use the Partial Offset Principle, to make the fullest use of the hotplates and to give complete control. Once boiling, even if a pan is only making partial contact with a hotplate, it will continue to boil. Provided your existing saucepans have heavy and perfectly flat bases, they should also give good results on an Aga. All too often the bases have ridges or concentric rings which limit the contact made. For a quick test, place a utensil on the Simmering Plate and see if it rocks at all. With cast-iron utensils, do check that the bases are not merely flat, with a rough casting surface, but that they are machine ground perfectly flat. Examine an Aga cast-iron ground base and compare with other makes and it is immediately obvious why the machined surface is the type which makes perfect contact. Similarly, a cast-iron utensil with a lip around the edge of the base renders it useless for cooking on a hotplate or on the floor of the Roasting Oven.

POOR

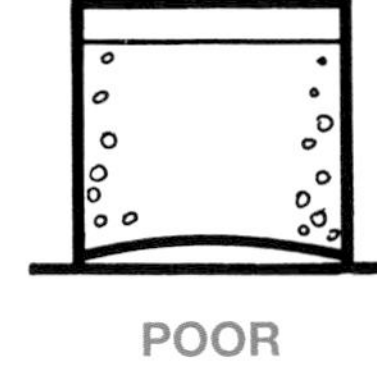

POOR

POOR

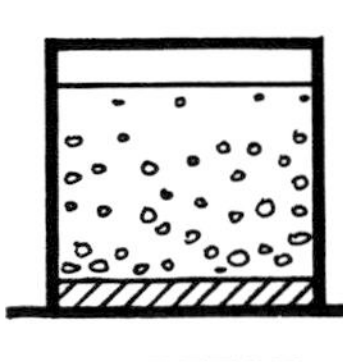

PERFECT

FLAT LIDS FOR MAXIMUM FLEXIBILITY

The final feature which makes Aga utensils essential is that the lids have recessed handles to facilitate stacking in the Simmering Oven. The range of Aga pans has also been specially designed to permit the maximum use of the Simmering Oven in many different pan combinations so that up to seven pans can be placed there at the same time.
This means that you will get the very best out of your cooker. Get into the habit of using your Simmering Oven to its fullest capacity from day one and you will immediately enjoy the best results from your Aga.

INVEST IN THE BEST

All Aga cookware is made to a very high standard and really is worth the investment. You have the world's finest cooker – you deserve to cook with the finest cookware. It is the the only range of utensils on the market which are specially designed and made for use with Aga cookers and will also last for many years. Indeed I have a number of Aga saucepans from the 40's, 50's and 60's and they still work as well today as the day they were bought by my grandparents. Only if you have Aga utensils can an Aga fully give the remarkable performance for which it is famous. As with knives, you get what you pay for. 'Buy cheap, buy twice' is a true maxim when buying kitchen equipment.

Your local Aga Specialist would be pleased to show you the complete range and help you in choosing what would be best for you. As I said in the introduction, I think it is best to build up slowly a collection of cookware so that you have a collection of pans which exactly suits your cooking, home and lifestyle. If you cook a lot of pasta, then a large pan such as the stockpot may well be a must. If you hardly eat pasta or make stock, your money may well be better spent on something else.

BUILD FROM ONE PAN

Owners are sometimes reluctant to purchase new cookware. All I can say is please buy one Aga pan and see for yourself. If you are starting with just one pan, then I would suggest a shallow pan with a broad base as being the most useful. With a large surface area making contact with the hotplates, this will give the most rapid boiling, perfect for bringing food quickly to the boil when you are in a hurry. For example boiling green vegetables just before serving a large meal. The first time I used an Aga pan it was a revelation. It was immediately obvious that its performance was far superior to that of my existing pans. As soon as I saw the immediate benefits, I started to build up my own collection and have never looked back.

KETTLES

Every time you switch on an electric kettle it is the same as turning on a three-bar electric fire – not cheap. Investing in an Aga kettle is therefore essential and will save you a lot of money by using the Aga's stored heat. A good Aga kettle will also boil more quickly than most electric kettles. I recommend the aluminium type as they boil the fastest. One with a good base on a clean Boiling Plate at full temperature will boil at the rate of a pint a minute. Modern Aga kettles are available in plain and hard anodised aluminium, some with a non-stick internal coating.

Always place your kettle on the hotplate with a slight twisting action to ensure perfect contact, this helps the kettle to 'bed in' if there happen to be any errant toast crumbs and ensures the best possible contact. Keep your hotplates spotless by brushing with the wire brush supplied with your Aga. Absolutely clean hotplates are essential to ensure efficient heat transfer. I particularly like the Classic Aga hotplate brush, as it is easy to hold when brushing the hotplates. With this it is easy to get into the habit of regularly making sure there are no deposits and you will then always have startling performance from your Boiling Plate. When making tea and coffee, always use freshly drawn water as this is oxygenated and therefore not 'flat'. Only fill as much as you need for the fastest boiling. You will find that in most cases, by the time you have assembled the tea tray and filled up the milk jug, the kettle will have already boiled. Try and avoid the practice of 'topping up' water in your kettle which then keeps on being re-boiled. This practice encourages the concentration of impurities and consequent formation of scale which can cause premature pitting of the metal. Because water can boil so quickly, there is normally little benefit in keeping a kettle full of hot water at the back of your Aga ready for use. Over time this too can cause damage, so empty it last thing and place to dry near the cooker. Of course when cooking a meal, it is perfectly acceptable to boil a kettle a short while ahead of time ready for pouring into a saucepan to bring back to a rapid boil – for example when cooking green vegetables.

If you place the spout facing the hotplate lid, the steam will also help to keep it clean, just an occasional wipe will keep it pristine. To keep your kettle at optimum boiling performance, get into the habit of regularly de-scaling it with an approved product. Aga cast-iron trivets are really useful. Use one to park your hot kettle and several more are also invaluable for protecting work surfaces from hot trays emerging from the oven.

STANDARD AGA KIT

The 'standard kit' supplied with every new Aga includes two grid shelves (three with the 3 oven). If you only have one, an extra one is advisable. Also standard is one solid cold plain shelf, which is an important piece of equipment as it is used in certain situations to provide a moderate baking temperature in the Roasting Oven. This is essential when baking in a 2 oven Aga. I think having at least one more is a wise purchase with all models. If you think you haven't got a cold plain shelf, do check the floors of your ovens as there may well be one sitting there without you realising. The wire toaster and full and half size Aga roasting tins come as standard, together with reversible grill racks. These are essential used in the high position for oven grilling at the top of the Roasting Oven and useful when set in the low position when roasting meat and poultry. The excellent Aga Book, a long-handled wire brush, a sample of some Aga cleaning paste and the new Aga owner's video guide are also supplied with a new Aga.

Because owners often take their Aga cookware with them when they move (this is a very common problem, as your local Aga Specialist will tell you) Aga have sensibly put together a starter pack for inherited Aga owners. It is attractively priced giving a significant saving over buying the above items separately.

I also suggest buying at least a second half size roasting tin and possibly a full size one as well. The small one, as well as being used for meat and poultry, makes a useful 'carrier' for other dishes, such as when making a baked milk pudding – any milk that boils over is contained, which makes cleaning up really simple. For the easiest cleaning, line the tin with a pre-cut piece of Bake-O-Glide (*see* page 49). A second full size roasting tin is particularly useful at Christmas. Once the turkey or goose is cooked, the bird can be carefully transferred to a clean roasting tin to rest. The fat and delicious congealed juices from the original tin can then be de-glazed to make wonderful gravy and any juices that collect from the resting bird can also be added to the flavour-packed sauce just before serving.

CAST IRON

Round Grill Pan

The round cast iron grill pan is good value and fantastic for steaks, chops and cutlets; it is also excellent for sardines and scallops. Cast iron is the best material for a grill pan and is my recommendation. If you find it too heavy, use both hands as there is a smaller second handle opposite the main one. A lighter aluminium version is also available which gives good results but the cast iron one does have the edge on performance.

Casseroles

I think at least one is useful and I prefer the oval type as they make the best use of space when they are transferred to the Simmering Oven for slow cooking. Choose a size appropriate for your family, useful for one-pot meals. The larger type can take a chicken or joint for a tasty pot roast and the flat lid means stacking is possible.

Danish Pot

A brilliant little pot – an absolute gem. Use it to make a quick rustic soup from surplus vegetables cooked with stock. A wand blender can then be used to purée it in the pan, saving on washing up.

Baking and Gratin Dishes

I use these a good deal as they are so versatile. They are ideal for quick supper dishes such as chicken breasts baked with a sauce or sautéed diced cooked potatoes. Being enamelled, they are smart enough to send to table, and are perfect for serving different delicious vegetable gratins, braised vegetables and layered potato side dishes.

Sauté Pan and Lid

My first choice for a sauté pan is cast aluminium, but the cast-iron one is a good second choice if you want something that is also smart enough for everyday table use.

STAINLESS STEEL

If you want pans that are able to be washed in a dishwasher, the stainless steel range is the one for you. The 3 piece saucepan and casserole sets are particularly good buys because you save money over buying the pans separately and also the two sets together fit neatly in the Simmering Oven.

3-Piece Saucepan Set

This set of pans fits together with the sister casserole set in the Simmering Oven. As well as their obvious use for making sauces, I personally prefer saucepans over casseroles when boiling and steaming vegetables as I think it is easier and safer to have the longer handle when draining off the water.

3-Piece Casserole Set

This set of pans fits together with the sister saucepan set in the Simmering Oven. Where no draining is involved, I personally prefer the casserole design when cooking in the Simmering Oven as the smaller side handles make stacking easier in the oven.

Shallow Saucepans and Casseroles with Lids
Broad-based utensils make for efficient heating with their large surface area making contact with the hotplates. I particularly like the 1.5 litre shallow saucepan with lid. They are so useful I keep two if not three to hand and recommend them highly. These are perfect for heating milk, making sauces, re-heating small amounts, and keeping sauces hot in the Warming and Simmering Ovens. The 2 litre shallow casserole and lid and 3 litre sauté casserole similarly heat up particularly quickly.

Saucepans and Casseroles
Select your choice of larger saucepans and casseroles, keeping in mind the size of your family and type of cooking, to augment the 3-piece sets.

Stockpot and Preserving Pan
The 9 litre tall stockpot is also for me a must-have as it boils so quickly, making it perfect for pasta. When it is full of water the weight bears down hard on the Boiling Plate resulting in an extremely rapid boil. Pasta should always be cooked in lots of water in a large pan. The stockpot also fits in the Simmering Oven.

As an alternative, consider the larger 11 litre preserving pan. As well as for making jams and chutneys, it is brilliant for making large batches of stock, chilli and Bolognaise type sauces.

HARD ANODISED ALUMINIUM

I like the stainless steel range very much, however they are not quite as rapid as aluminium, which after silver is the best conductor of heat. There is a trade-off from ultimate boiling with the ease of washing in the dishwasher. Stainless steel is my first choice for most purposes – a range of cookware which does feature a thick aluminium sandwich within the base to give the best possible heat conduction. However, aluminium helps produce the very fastest boiling and I like to use an aluminium pan for some things, especially when rapidly boiling green vegetables. The 3-piece saucepan and casserole sets are again good buys, because you save money over buying the pans separately.

3 Piece Saucepan and 3 Piece Casserole Sets
These sets are worth considering but it should be noted that, unlike the two stainless steel sets, not all six of these can fit together in the Simmering Oven at the same time. I would plump for one or other set; I particularly like the casserole set as it includes the shallow 3.5 litre casserole which is an excellent pan for many purposes. Alternatively, choose the 3-piece saucepan set and augment that with two 3.5 litre shallow casseroles. Two of these will sit on top of each other and as well as being great for potatoes and root vegetables, they are big enough for browning meat and then adding ingredients to make casseroles. Their broad bases help produce extremely rapid boiling.

Shallow Saucepan with Lids

Broad-based utensils make for efficient heating with the large surface area making contact with the hotplates. As with the stainless steel version, I like the 1.5 litre saucepan with lid. If you prefer aluminium to stainless steel, keep at least two if not three to hand as you will find them invaluable.

Saucepans and Casseroles

As with the stainless steel range, select your choice of larger saucepans and casseroles to suit your size of family and type of cooking.

Large Aga Wok

I thoroughly recommend the large hard anodised aluminium Aga wok. For the best results, make sure your hotplates are absolutely clean – use a wire brush to ensure good contact. Pre-heat the wok thoroughly before use for a couple of minutes on the Simmering Plate to save the intense heat stored in the fast Boiling Plate for the actual cooking. If you have been using the Boiling Plate for several things beforehand, it is best to allow a short time for it to return to its highest heat, by leaving the lid closed. Transfer the pre-heated wok to the Boiling Plate and after a couple of minutes add your chosen oil. Wait until the oil shows a rippling pattern and is good and hot, add the initial ingredients and get sizzling. Keep the wok flat on the hotplate during cooking and use two wooden spatulas to keep the mixture moving.

CAST ALUMINIUM

Frying and Sauté Pans

These multi-purpose pans are fantastic for genuine non-stick cooking. You need hardly any oil or fat so they are great for healthy cooking. The removable handle means that they can be transferred to the floor of the Roasting Oven or into the Simmering Oven to continue cooking.

Casseroles and Skillet Lids

These are particularly useful when making casseroles, as floured meat can be browned in batches and then kept warm in the upturned lid. After softening onions and garlic, return the meat to the pan and add the rest of the ingredients. At other times the lid can also be used to serve a vegetable or side dish.

Baking Dish

This is the one oven dish that can be used for roasting and then may be used on the Boiling Plate to make gravy or a sauce without any danger of the base becoming damaged. It is particularly useful for enjoying suppers such as baked chicken breast and thigh recipes.

BAKEWARE

Roasting Tins and Grill Racks

As we have seen, Aga roasting tins fit directly on the oven runners and if you purchase some extras you will find that you use them for many different everyday things. Two half size tins will fit one in front of the other. Plain or hard anodised aluminium, enamelled and stainless steel versions are available in both sizes. Deeper turkey or straight sided variants are also available from time to time. The grill racks for the roasting tins are a comparatively recent introduction, so if you have an older cooker you would benefit from these as they make oven grilling much quicker as well as being useful when roasting meat or poultry which is particularly fatty and needs draining as it cooks.

Baking Trays

Apart from treating yourself to some extra roasting tins, the other most important oven accessories that I find absolutely invaluable are Aga baking trays. These are made of hard anodised aluminium and come in half and full sizes. As with the Aga roasting tins, they fit the oven runners and are extremely versatile. Because of their substantial but surprisingly light construction, there is no danger of them warping in the hot ovens as can happen with cheap bakeware. Several of the half size trays are useful for baking or steaming so many things, and they are invaluable used as a carrier for other things, from home-made dishes to hastily-cooked ready-meals. I find having two of the half size ones enough for normal everyday cooking, together with two half size roasting tins. The full size trays are the real multi-purpose stars, however. I like these so much, in fact, that I now have a set of four in my kitchen. They are endlessly put to use; once you buy one you will end up wanting more!

Perfect for so many items, I most often press baking trays into service when cooking large quantities of roast potatoes and parsnips and other root vegetables. In recent years, roasted Mediterranean vegetables have become a common ingredient in a lot of contemporary recipes and again these trays make light work of cooking a large quantity. They are invaluable at Christmas too. For example, if cooking a large roast meal on a 2 oven Aga, once the turkey is having its all-important rest before being carved, four large trays can all be accommodated in the Roasting Oven at the same time. Two trays of roast potatoes, one on the oven floor and one just above, can be swapped a couple of times so that they all enjoy a spell on the oven floor. Above these can be a tray of cocktail sausages roasting perhaps with maple syrup alongside some stuffing balls and then a whole tray of bacon rolls and the like can be grilled at the very top of the oven.

They are also invaluable for baking or re-heating large quantities of canapés and nibbles. All the preparation can be done ahead of time and the trays effortlessly slid into the oven and timed for six or seven minutes before serving. The other recipes that I most use the full sized trays are for baking all kinds of large desserts including impressive roulades. Plain, hazelnut, chocolate, meringue – they are all quickly made and produce impressive buffet table desserts in a very short time.

THE AGA CAKE BAKER: A UNIVERSAL PAN

With a 2 oven Aga, if you want to bake large, deep cakes that require more than 45 minutes' cooking at a moderate temperature, an Aga Cake Baker is a great investment. Once pre-heated, it maintains a centre temperature the same as the Baking Oven on a 3 and 4 oven cooker. Foods requiring a high temperature can be cooked at the same time elsewhere in the Roasting Oven. As well as making an 'oven within an oven', it is a really useful 9 pint (5 litre) universal pan that can be routinely used for boiling pasta and rice, making everyday batches of stock, Bolognaise sauces, Ragùs, curries and chillis. It is also great for boiling hams and chickens and doubling up batches of your favourite casserole recipes. With its heavy base, the Cake Baker also serves as an excellent medium-sized preserving pan. The flat lid means that you can stack things on top of it in the Simmering Oven and the internal trivet also makes it my favourite choice for cooking steamed puddings, both sweet and savoury. Think of it as an everyday saucepan. Just keep the carrier and cake tins on the shelf in the cupboard. You will find it will become one of your favourite utensils.

OTHER BAKEWARE

By all means use all your existing bakeware in the Aga. However, the Roasting Oven is very hot and I would recommend you choose Aga bakeware as and when you replace items. This is because they are very heavily made, specifically to withstand the high temperatures and thus provide many years of use without warping. The unique design is made in a dark colour so that they absorb heat more quickly which gives a 10% saving in energy by shortening cooking times and ensuring even and dependable browning with no burning or hot spots.

Apart from the roasting tins and baking trays, the other most popular items are the deep muffin and mini muffin tins. These give very good results for small sponge cakes and muffins and the mini tins are great for baby Yorkshire puddings which make wonderful canapés (*see* page 132). They are also useful for making croustades, petits fours and mini mince pies at Christmas – much nicer than offering yet more of the normal size when everyone is feeling full.

4-Way Timer

Because the ovens are vented, your kitchen stays largely free from cooking smells. This does, however, mean it is possible to forget something, so a kitchen timer is an absolute must. The 4-way digital timer from Aga works well and has a different beep for each timer. It will stand on a worktop, is magnetic for a refrigerator door or can be clipped to your clothing if you leave the kitchen to do something else.

Classic Baker's Paddle

This is invaluable for inserting rustic loaves of bread directly onto the floor of the Roasting Oven. It is also perfect as a pizza peel for manoeuvring pizzas in and out of the oven easily. Dust with a little cornmeal before using, so that dough doesn't stick when you slide the paddle away.

Bake-O-Glide

Bake-O-Glide is a reusable non-stick coated cooking liner. Available in a range of packs, the Aga Cook Set is the most versatile. It contains pre-cut pieces with mitre-cut corners to fit the half and full size roasting tins and shapes to fit the plain shelf of the Simmering Plate. The latter is useful when making quick cheese on toast for one or toasted sandwiches, as it makes cleaning up any mess really easy. Although it can be used for drop scones, I prefer the finish when these are cooked directly on the Simmering Plate. However, if you are using a solid fuel Aga, it is then useful for this purpose as it covers the whole hotplate including the centre removable flue-cleaning plug. Bake-O-Glide is an Aga essential, a product that really is as good as it claims to be. You don't have to use it when cooking on an Aga, it just makes good sense. I find it extremely useful for a lot of things, but not every lining purpose (see below). It is very durable and if looked after it will last for many years – I have several pieces that are now more than 12 years old and they are still in daily use at home. Over time they will darken but this does not affect their performance. For most purposes it can be used untreated for totally non-stick cooking.

For other recipes, only very small quantities of oil or fat need to be used, so it is also ideal for virtually fat-free cooking. For the Simmering Plate circle only, you need to prepare the circle before it is suitable for cooking the famous Aga fat-free fried egg. Simply wipe both sides lightly with a little sunflower or vegetable oil using a piece of kitchen paper. This very small amount of oil will season it, and you will never have to do this again. This is an important little trick you can now knowingly pass on to other Aga-owning friends who wonder why their egg stuck when they tried it at home! This is not necessary for any of the other pieces or for any other purpose. As well as the Cook Set, the small liner is available for use on the plain shelf. The large liner is designed to be cut up to fit your other favourite bakeware items and make having to prepare parchment cake tin liners a thing of the past. There is even a Cake Baker set with different sized disks and strips to line the three tins which come with this piece of equipment. To clean Bake-O-Glide, wash in warm soapy water, rinse and then dry with a tea towel. It can also be washed in a dishwasher, by simply placing pieces in-between dinner plates in the lower rack to prevent them from fouling the rotating spray arms.

A word of warning – there are two ways to lose Bake-O-Glide (or three if you include family members throwing it away!). Firstly it is safe everywhere in and on your Aga apart from the intense heat of the Boiling Plate. Secondly, it can be damaged if you cut down onto it with a sharp kitchen knife. So if you are dividing up something like shortbread or flapjack in a tin, use a blunt table knife and you will do no damage.

KitchenAid Mixer

Although not an Aga piece of equipment, many Aga owners purchase these mixers as their planetary action is fantastic for mixing cake mixtures, whisking egg whites and whipping cream.

The dough hook is perfect for kneading bread, and paired with the Aga Roasting Oven it makes home bread-making really easy. If you would like to get into the habit of making bread with your Aga on a regular basis, I would certainly recommend you consider putting one of these on your wish list.

To see how easy this is, *see* Daily Bread, page 65.

TEXTILES

Gauntlets, Aprons and Oven Gloves

The attention to detail with Aga extends even to the superior design of the textile range. The extra long gauntlets and oven gloves incorporate an ingenious integral steam and grease barrier, as well as excellent insulation to protect your arms when reaching into the depths of the ovens (these ovens are deep and can contain a lot of food: you risk a glancing burn without any protection). I consider these an absolute must and, personally, prefer the gauntlets over the oven gloves. Gauntlets are best used in pairs when lifting hot roasting tins and trays. A wide range of other mitts and protective wear is also available, made to the same high specification. I also consider the aprons a must.

Chef's Pads

These are essential to protect the metal or enamel surface on your insulated lids. The newer type are reversible, cream on one side and black on the other.

NON-AGA EQUIPMENT AND ACCESSORIES

Baking Parchment

I still find uses for silicone baking parchment when baking, where I prefer it to using Bake-O-Glide. Baking parchment is the modern replacement for greaseproof paper and I like to use it when lining a tin for a roulade or Swiss roll. It is easier to get the parchment folded sharply to fit the base and sides of the tin neatly. Always oil the inside of a tin first then the parchment will adhere to the tin easily.

I also prefer using a large piece of parchment for turning a baked swiss roll onto before allowing it to cool and rolling it up.

Aluminium Foil

People are often unsure if foil can be used in the Aga. It certainly can, and the most common use for it is for 'tenting' a turkey or goose at Christmas. As with any cooker, it is ideal for protecting food but it does not have the profound shielding effect of inserting a cold plain shelf above food. It is certainly useful for protecting vulnerable parts of poultry which could otherwise overcook prematurely, such as wing tips. I also enjoy using it to cook en papilotte, where a circle of foil or parchment is filled with a delicate food, a mere drizzle of cooking liquid such as wine, and then the whole folded over and the edge strongly crimped closed, to form a large foil pasty shape. A number of these can then be baked on a plain shelf or baking tray in the Roasting Oven for a short time with perfect results. Follow the method and cooking times recommended for this technique given in any cook book. Foil is also used with parchment to cover steamed puddings. Make a pleat in both pieces to allow for the mixture to expand when cooking.

Clingfilm

Clingfilm can be used in the Simmering and Warming Ovens. This is useful for covering food, especially for covering jugs of sauces which are not being stored in covered saucepans, but are needed to be kept hot.

Pyrex

Pyrex jugs are extremely useful and take up little space in the Simmering Oven. Because they can be used for so many things, and to allow for some being full of food or in the dishwasher, I have half a dozen of the pint size and several of the larger type in my kitchen. Milk can be measured and left to warm through in the Simmering Oven for half an hour, ready for swiftly incorporating into a roux when making a Béchamel type sauce. Sauces can be made ahead of time and then transferred to jugs and covered with clingfilm to keep hot until wanted in the Warming or Simmering Oven. This means that saucepans can be washed and put away before guests arrive. After use, the empty jugs will then take little space in a dishwasher when clearing up at the end of a meal. Larger jugs can obviously be used for larger quantities; two will fit on top of each other in the Simmering Oven using a suitably-sized plate as a spacer. Pyrex plates and baking dishes can also be used in all of the Aga ovens with complete success.

Plastic Containers

Anything that is plastic and dishwasher-safe is safe in the Simmering and Warming Ovens. Plastic jugs and pudding basins may also be used.

Post-it Notes and Notepads

Keep a supply of bright stickers or Post-it notes by your Aga. If you think you might forget something cooking in an oven, place one on the oven door as a visual reminder. I also leave messages for myself on notepads if cooking something slowly over many hours, such as 'don't forget stock' or 'take out steak and kidney mixture at 8 o'clock', as otherwise it is easy to forget something.

3. GOOD FOOD FAST

Having an Aga in your kitchen means it is easy to cook good, simple food really fast. With busy lives, none of us consistently have the time to be cooking great production numbers, especially mid-week. What's needed is simple, uncomplicated food, prepared in next to no time. With its immediacy and simplicity, the Aga makes this really easy. When friends visit, they will be impressed at the speed at which you can rustle up something simple that tastes absolutely delicious. With just a few easy preparations in place, you can even produce freshly baked biscuits, cakes or drop scones – all in a matter of minutes. For something more substantial, the intense heat of the Roasting Oven makes short work of all-day breakfasts and everyday convenience foods and can even provide you with freshly-baked bread in no more than ten minutes. That's what Good Food Fast means for today's Aga cook. In this section, I share some simple key techniques for producing good, wholesome food in double-quick time.

WELL BEGUN IS HALF DONE

The immediate readiness of the Aga means that by keeping some equipment and a few ingredients ready-prepared in your kitchen, you can very quickly produce something delicious. Some things which take the longest to prepare can be kept pre-prepared in your kitchen cupboards together with having a well-stocked refrigerator and freezer. Here are some ideas to get you started:

EASY BAKING GET AHEADS

SWISS ROLL

Keep a Swiss roll tin lined and greased and store in a polythene bag. The ingredients, 3 oz (75g) of both caster sugar and sieved self-raising flour, can be weighed and stored in plastic bags or boxes with a 13 x 9 inch (33 x 23cm) cake tin. In this way a store-cupboard cake can be produced in minutes for unexpected guests. Whisk the warmed sugar with 3 large eggs until pale and foamy. Fold in the flour, pour into the tin and then cook for 7 minutes on a grid shelf on the floor of the Roasting Oven. While the cake cooks, place a jar of jam in the Simmering Oven with its lid loosened ready for filling the turned out cake.

SCONES

Keep your favourite scone mixture weighed out in the refrigerator, ready for mixing with milk and egg in a matter of moments. Rub the fat into the self-raising flour and baking powder, add sugar and sultanas and store the mixture in a box in the freezer. When wanted, place in a bowl and add a beaten egg and enough milk to bind. Work lightly to a slightly sticky mixture for the lightest results and pat into a diamond shape on a piece of Bake-O-Glide on a plain shelf. Use a palette knife to fashion into smaller diamonds and separate out with no waste. Brush with milk and bake for 8-10 minutes on the third set of runners in the Roasting Oven. Savoury cheese mixtures benefit from a little dry English mustard powder, which helps to bring out the depth of the cheese's flavour.

CAKE MIXTURES

Keep a favourite cake mixture ready weighed out in a plastic bag or box in the refrigerator, with a label listing the wet ingredients which need to be added and the Aga baking position. All-in-one mixtures which use soft baking margarine are my favourites. Drop the margarine into a KitchenAid with the dry ingredients and any liquid required. Use the mixing beater and beat for 30 seconds, scrape down and beat for a further 10 seconds. The pre-cut Bake-O-Glide liners for the roasting tins complete this express technique. If any topping is required, this can be added to the cooled cake in the tin whilst it is setting.

DROP SCONE MIXTURES

For almost instant Scotch pancakes, keep the sieved flour ready-weighed out in an airtight container. Use 4 oz (100g) of self-raising flour and add a tablespoon of caster sugar if making sweet ones. When hungry friends drop by, just add an egg and approximately 1/4 pint (150ml) of milk to make a batter the consistency of single cream. Pour spoonfuls onto the greased Simmering Plate and you can offer your guests piping hot scones in less than two minutes. Keep a warm plate on a folded tea towel on the closed Boiling Plate lid when making drop scones, Welshcakes, pikelets and crumpets. You can then keep your freshly made fare hot whilst you finish the batch. Cover with the end of the tea towel to prevent them drying out.

PANCAKES AND CREPES

Use the same recipe as drop scones for pancakes, but use plain flour and twice the amount of milk to make a thinner batter. Next time you want to make pancakes, cook each one in an oiled omelette pan on the Boiling Plate and then turn out onto the greased Simmering Plate to finish off the other side. You can then start on the next pancake while the first gets completed on the Simmering Plate. Alternatively, for crêpes, spread the batter out on the Simmering Plate using the back of a spoon.

REFRIGERATOR BISCUITS

Follow the normal recipes and then roll into 2 inch (5cm) cylinders. Wrap tightly in clingfilm and then store in the refrigerator or freezer. When fresh biscuits are wanted, simply unwrap and slice into disks and place, well spaced apart, onto a piece of Bake-O-Glide on a cold plain shelf. Bake as directed in the baking section and cool on wire trays. If you possess a biscuit press (similar to an icing syringe, but much larger), these mixtures can be kept for several days in the press in the refrigerator with the end tightly covered. Fresh shapes can be extruded onto Bake-O-Glide on a cold plain shelf for baking in a similar way as required.

EASY MEAL GET AHEADS

FLAN IN A FLURRY

When you are next making something with short-crust pastry, make a larger batch and line a couple of extra flan tins. Prick the bases and then store in plastic bags in the freezer. When a tasty light lunch is wanted, whisk together 3 eggs with $^1/_2$ pint (300ml) of single or double cream. Certain dairy substitutes from the chiller cabinet available today have long-life refrigerator times. Season with freshly ground black pepper and salt, perhaps with a little freshly grated nutmeg. Half-fill the pastry base with your chosen filling – a freezer or tinned staple such as prawns or crumbled crabmeat, or some leftover cooked ham. Pour over the cream mixture and add a little cheese. Cook directly on the floor of the Roasting Oven for 20-30 minutes.

SOUP SECRETS

When making home-made soup, if you have some left that won't be needed the next day, freeze it in a shallow, broad-based Aga pan. A few hours later, when it is just solid, take it out of the freezer and hold the pan for a few seconds upside down under a hot tap. The soup will come out in one lump ready for storing in a plastic bag, leaving the pan free for other uses. When soup is wanted at short notice, return it to the same pan and place on the Simmering Plate, covered. It will defrost and re-heat extremely quickly, needing only an occasional stir over 7-10 minutes. Bake some frozen rolls at the same time to serve with the soup.

PANCAKES AT THE DOUBLE

Keep a batch of ready-made pancakes in the freezer, interleaved with baking parchment and wrapped tightly in foil. These may be reheated one at a time from frozen on one side only on a lightly greased Simmering Plate ready for filling with a savoury filling and sauce.

CRUMBLE TOPPINGS

Savoury and sweet crumble toppings can be made in the normal way, rubbing fat into flour and then adding grated cheese and seasoning or demerara sugar and spice. Store in the freezer for topping dishes quickly to cook fast in the Roasting or Baking Ovens.

THE FAMOUS AGA BREAKFAST

A full cooked English breakfast is an occasional treat for most of us, and it is as easy to prepare for one or two, as for twenty-two with the Aga ovens at your disposal. For some things you can't beat frying in just a little fat, but for others I insist on grilling. Both ways are so easy, the choice is yours. Use Aga roasting tins and baking trays to cook a lot of food simultaneously. If I am cooking for smaller numbers I particularly like to use a small grill rack in the high position at one end of a full size roasting tin as I can then use the other end for access to foods cooking. Here is my favourite 'breakfast for two' which can even be prepared the night before so that there is very little to do in the morning:

BREAKFAST FOR TWO

Line a full size Aga roasting tin with Bake-O-Glide. At one end, place two halved tomatoes: cut them around their circumference, and slice a sliver off their bases so that they sit without wobbling. Next to them place some sliced mushrooms. Season with salt and freshly ground black pepper, and a grate of nutmeg over the mushrooms. Over this, place a half size grill rack and add four sausages (at this point you can cover with clingfilm and place the tin in your refrigerator if you wish). Slide the tin onto the top set of runners to grill the sausages, tomatoes and mushrooms. No extra fat will be needed. After 8-10 minutes, turn the sausages, which will have browned. After a further 5-8 minutes, move the sausages down to sit next to the tomatoes and mushrooms, and add 4-6 rashers of dry cured bacon to the grill rack. Return to the very top of the oven and as the bacon cooks, the delicious juices will drop down to season the mushrooms and tomatoes. Now make four pieces of toast using the Boiling Plate and use a 3 inch (8cm) scone cutter to cut out circles in two of them. Turn the bacon – I prefer grilled bacon quite soft, with the edges only just starting to brown, but of course you can cook it more if you wish. If you prefer really crisp streaky bacon, cook on a tray on the floor of the oven. When the bacon is almost how you like it, add the two toast frames to the Bake-O-Glide and crack a free-range egg into each frame. Return the tin to the oven floor to fry the eggs, they will take 2-3 minutes. Serve on warm plates from the Simmering Oven with the rest of the toast.

FRIED EGGS

I prefer the healthier fried egg in toast to fried bread, but by adding a little oil first, delicious fried bread can be made. Just add the bread earlier in proceedings to cook in the oil in the oven, turning once. It will not be as greasy as when shallow fried. As an alternative to frying the eggs in the oven, you can cook fat-free fried eggs on a circle of Bake-O-Glide on the Simmering Plate, with the lid lowered.

SCRAMBLED EGGS

Scrambled eggs are best made using a non-stick pan. Melt the butter in it first on the Simmering Plate and then add the eggs beaten with a little milk and salt and freshly ground black pepper. Use a flat-ended wooden spatula to stir the cooked curds away from the base of the pan as they form. When they are half-cooked, it is also possible to transfer the covered pan to the Simmering Oven to finish cooking. Stir in a little extra cold butter or chilled cream at the end to arrest the cooking so that they don't over-cook.

POACHED EGGS

Poached eggs are easy using the Partial Offset Principle. The secret of success is using really fresh eggs. These will not spread and no salt or vinegar will need to be added to the water. Use a shallow pan which can be filled about an inch (2.5cm) full of boiling water. I use a non-stick cast aluminium sauté pan or similar. Position it half on the Simmering Plate so there is the barest shimmer of movement from the still surface. Crack the eggs into the water, using a cup first if you prefer. Cook for 3-4 minutes and remove using a slotted spoon.

BREAKFAST FOR A CROWD

The same principles can be used for cooking a breakfast for large numbers. I find that Aga baking trays are the answer here as well as using a couple of full size roasting tins. A whole tray can be devoted to each different food, using the different heat zones in the Roasting Oven. Grill bacon at the very top and fry sausages on a tray on the floor, with tomatoes and mushrooms in-between. Obviously other ingredients such as black pudding can be similarly cooked. If you are grilling a lot of sausages on a 3 or 4 oven Aga, use the same method but cook these at the very top of the Baking Oven, allowing a little longer. With crowds it is best to fry the eggs at the last minute on a baking tray on the floor of the oven, either using the toast frame (see 'Breakfast for Two') or with the eggs loose. A tip here is to crack the eggs ahead of time onto a dinner plate and then they can be gently tipped into the tray of hot fat all in one go so that they all cook at the same rate. With fresh eggs they will keep separate. For scrambled or poached eggs, cook as above.

OTHER BREAKFAST OPTIONS

Poach kippers and smoked haddock in the Baking or Roasting Oven. Pour over a little boiling water in an Aga roasting tin, and leave for 5-8 minutes in the middle of the oven until just cooked. Once tinned tomatoes and baked beans have been heated through, they may be kept hot for hours in the Simmering Oven without drying out. Freshly sautéed mushrooms may also be cooked ahead of time and served as required. Cooked sausages also keep well here without drying out, and even batches of scrambled egg can be kept for a short time between orders without deteriorating.

BREAKFAST SIDE DISHES

To complement the cooked breakfasts, here are some of my other favourite breakfast dishes and instructions on how to cook them to perfection on the Aga.

PERFECT AGA PORRIDGE

Aga porridge is legendary. For authentic overnight Aga porridge you need to use oatmeal, not rolled oats. If you have difficulty in obtaining them from a supermarket (they are stocked in most places these days), try a health food shop. Traditional recipes suggest using medium pinhead oatmeal. I prefer to use half medium and half fine ground. Both are much cheaper than rolled oats.

It is important to use a cooking pan that has a good lid, to ensure that no liquid can be driven off over the long slow cooking causing the porridge to dry out. I use an Aga stainless steel pan and like to place a piece of wetted baking parchment over the pot before pressing down the lid to ensure an extra-tight seal. Last thing at night, or perhaps while making any bedtime drinks, bring a pint (600 ml) of water to the boil in a heavy based pan with a pinch of salt, and stir in 3 oz (75 g) of medium pinhead oatmeal. Simmer on the Simmering Plate for a couple of minutes, and then cover with a tight-fitting lid and transfer to a position low down in the coolest oven on your cooker, on a grid shelf or Aga toaster and leave overnight. Serve with a little more salt to taste or sweeten with golden or maple syrup and offer creamy milk at the table. Some people like to stir in dried fruits but I prefer those separately.

In my opinion, Aga porridge is far superior when made with oatmeal, but you can also make porridge in the Aga using rolled oats. Simply mix it up the night before and leave the pan covered at the back of the top plate, or, on a 4 oven cooker, the Warming Plate. Leave it to cook slowly overnight.

FRUIT COMPOTES

Breakfast prunes lose half their terrors if the dried fruit is gently poached overnight in a mixture of half water and half apple juice or Earl Grey tea. Assemble and place in the Warming or Simmering Oven from cold. The gentle heat will cook the fruit to perfection. Similarly, dried apricots or mixed fruit salad can be coaxed to plump perfection for serving with Aga yoghurt (*see* page 83).

BREAKFAST PASTRIES

For the ultimate fresh continental breakfast, defrost some frozen croissants in the refrigerator overnight, covered with clingfilm and with the tail side facing downwards. They will prove slowly, ready to cook in just seven minutes low down in the Roasting Oven the following morning. Alternatively, place some ready-to-cook pains au chocolat covered with clingfilm in the refrigerator overnight. They will then be ready to cook in just seven minutes in the same position.

BREAKFAST CEREALS

Home-made granola style breakfast cereals can easily be made by drying out a well-tossed mixture of porridge oats, nuts and raisins, mixing in maple syrup and then leaving on Aga baking trays in the Simmering and Warming Ovens. Shake to toss the mixture every so often and then leave to finish drying out on a chef's pad on top of the closed insulated lids overnight. When perfectly dried, store in glass jars. Dried banana chips are best added just before storing.

DRIED FRUITS

Drying fruit for making homemade muesli-type cereals is easy using the Aga Warming and Simmering Ovens (*see* pages 32 and 35).

CONVENIENCE SNACKS

TOASTED SANDWICHES FOR ONE OR A CROWD

As well as toasting up to four toasted sandwiches on the Simmering Plate (*see* page 11), large quantities can be cooked at the same time on sheets of Bake-O-Glide on cold plain shelves. Nine assembled sandwiches fit each shelf and two shelves of sandwiches can be cooked at the same time. Slide one in at the very top of the Roasting Oven and the other directly onto the oven floor. Turn the top batch after 6-10 minutes. The lower ones will cook on both sides in the same time without needing turning.

CHEESE ON TOAST FOR ONE OR A CROWD

Easy cheese on toast for one is made using either a thin slice of cheese or grated cheese. Place this on a piece of medium-sliced bread and dust with a little paprika. Place in the middle of a piece of Bake-O-Glide on the Simmering Plate and lower the lid. In 2-3 minutes the bread will toast and the cheese melt in the heat from the lid. For a crowd, up to 18 slices can be cooked at the same time using the floor and top of the Roasting Oven. Assemble the first nine as above and place on Bake-O-Glide on a cold plain shelf on the floor of the oven. Now toast nine pieces of bread, on one side only, using the Aga toaster. Turn upside down and cover with cheese. Place these on Bake-O-Glide on a second cold plain shelf and slide in at the very top of the Roasting Oven.

PIZZAS TO GO FOR ONE OR A CROWD

The floor of the Roasting Oven can be used to cook home-made or bought fresh or frozen pizzas to perfection with a textbook crisp base. Use an Aga baker's paddle to make light work of moving them in and out of the oven. Lightly dust the paddle with cornmeal so that the dough will not stick to the paddle and will slip off easily onto the oven floor just like it does for the professionals. Two 10 inch (25cm) or three 7 inch (18cm) pizzas can fit at a time, front to back. Bake for 8-12 minutes. If making a lot of pizzas, the first batch can be transferred to the grid shelf at the top of the oven for the final five minutes while the next are started on the floor of the oven. On a 3 or 4 oven Aga, the floor of the Baking Oven may also be used, but they will take a little longer to cook. Pissaladière naturally is another star turn.

BAKED POTATOES

Baked potatoes in the Aga are fantastic. Scrub well and prick with a fork and wipe with a little oil if liked. Place in a single layer and cook directly on a grid shelf on the third set of runners in the Roasting Oven for $1^1/_4$-$1^1/_2$ hours, depending on size and quantity cooked. If baking more than one layer, a second layer above will act in the same way as a cold plain shelf, causing the lower layer to cook more slowly. Therefore allow 50% extra time and swap the two batches around half-way through cooking. If you are in a hurry, use thick aluminium skewers to help conduct the heat to the centre of the potatoes or cut them in half. To speed up the cooking even further, cover with boiling water and simmer on the Simmering Plate for 10 minutes. Remove, quickly pat dry, and prick well. Finish cooking on the grid shelf on the third set of runners of the Roasting Oven for about 30 minutes. Cooked baked potatoes will keep hot in the Simmering and Warming Ovens.

STIR-FRIES

Stir-fries are great for speedy, healthy meals. Ideally use the large hard anodised Aga wok, but a deep-sided sauté pan can also be used. It is vital that the pan is thoroughly pre-heated elsewhere on the Aga before it is added to the Boiling Plate. Then allow a good couple of minutes here to absorb fully the intense heat before adding your oil. When this shows a rippling pattern in the base of the pan and it is just about to smoke, add your initial ingredients. For some recipes it's a good idea to add aromatics such as sliced fresh ginger and garlic as soon as the oil is introduced to allow them to flavour the oil as it heats up. Remove them before they have a chance to burn and then add the main ingredients of the stir-fry.

STEAM-FRIES

For even healthier stir-fries, try their fat-free cousins, using twice the quantity of a well-flavoured vegetable stock in place of oil, and cover with a lid in-between stirring. Add more stock, a tablespoon at a time, if required while cooking, to prevent sticking.

PASTA FASTA

A lot of us eat pasta quite frequently these days and noodles also make a substantial quick meal, cooking in as little as 4 minutes. I recommend using a good quality dried Italian pasta for most purposes as the supermarket fresh types are not of a very good standard. If you want fresh pasta, make your own or purchase from a good family-run Italian delicatessen. Always use a large amount of boiling water in a large pan. Cooking pasta in too small a pan results in water that becomes over-saturated with starch and this can cause the pasta to stick. As a guide, use 8 pints (5 litres) of water for every 1 lb (500g) of pasta. Bring a large pan of water to the boil on the Boiling Plate – it may be quicker to do this by boiling an Aga kettle several times. If you know you will be returning home later in the day and will want to make a pasta meal in double-quick time, consider leaving a covered pan of hot water in the Simmering Oven. As soon as you arrive you can return it to the Boiling Plate and drop in the pasta as the water immediately boils. Either transfer to the Simmering Oven, or leave on the Boiling Plate, possibly partially offsetting the pan. Cook for the recommended cooking time while you make or re-heat a simple sauce.

OMELETTES

Use a 6 inch (15cm) omelette pan to make a classic 3-egg omelette. A 9 inch (23cm) pan will require 4-5 eggs. The smaller size is perfect for one person. Use three large fresh eggs, I would recommend using free-range. Place them in a small bowl, with a pinch of salt, a good grinding of black pepper and just a little freshly grated nutmeg. Add a generous tablespoon of water (not milk, as that tends to encourage a tough texture). Beat with a large table fork to combine the ingredients until they are all incorporated, but not too thoroughly – you want some discernible strands of yolk and white. Heat the dry omelette pan on the Boiling Plate for a good minute and then add a knob of butter. Swirl it around the pan, returning it to the heat and wait until the butter is just starting to turn a light nutty brown (noisette). Add the eggs and use the tines of the fork pointing upwards to stir the omelette gradually so that the uncooked mixture is gradually introduced to the base of the pan as the rest of the egg cooks and is pushed aside.

An alternative method is to use a sharp shaking action, moving the pan backwards and forwards with a jerk, to achieve the same effect. When the mixture is three-quarters cooked, add a filling. If a cold one, such as cheese, add and then transfer the pan to the very top of the Roasting Oven for a couple of minutes. This will melt the cheese and finish cooking the omelette. Alternatively, add the hot prepared filling and when the mixture is just cooked, turn deftly onto a hot plate, using two alternate folds to give the omelette a neat rolled-up presentation. Use a palette knife if necessary to help you. Send to the table immediately – omelettes wait for no man. The ideal centre texture of an omelette is baveuse, which denotes a lightly cooked effect, with the centre only just cooked. After you have made a few omelettes you will soon become proficient.

AGA DAILY BREAD

10 MINUTE BREAD

I recommend all Aga owners to keep supplies of part-baked petits pains and 12-inch baguettes for baking in just seven minutes for delicious fresh bread. These are sold in modified atmosphere packaging so they keep well at ambient temperature in a cool place such as a larder or pantry. They also freeze well and can be baked from frozen. Bake on the grid shelf on lowest set of runners in the Roasting Oven for 6-7 minutes or 10 minutes from frozen. With these in store an instant supply of warm bread is always possible, whether for a crowd or just a couple of people.

REJUVENATING BREAD

To revive a slightly stale loaf of bread, cut off a slice from the 'open' end of the loaf and discard. Hold the loaf, cut-side down, for a few moments under a running cold tap, and then place it in the Roasting Oven for four minutes to produce warm, crusty bread.

GET AHEAD BREAD

If you are a keen bread-maker, try freezing some risen bread dough in bread tins or as rolls as soon as proving has taken place. When frozen, store in plastic bags in the freezer until needed. Remove from the freezer and allow to defrost, then bake freshly in the Aga Roasting Oven as required. When baking bread throw an ice cube onto the floor of the oven just before shutting the oven door. The steam produced will ensure a perfect crust.

CONVENIENCE INGREDIENTS

If you like to use pre-prepared sauces purchased from the chiller cabinet in your supermarket such as cheese sauce, these can be heated through in their plastic tubs in the Simmering Oven ready for using hot with the dish you are preparing, saving washing up. Always open them first and then loosely replace the lid before heating. Allow 30-40 minutes for a small container and up to an hour for a large one.

CONVENIENCE MEALS

UNWRAP IT AND ZAP IT

To cook ready-meals follow the general cooking instructions, pricking or removing the clear film as instructed before cooking. Place on a baking tray or plain shelf and slide this onto a grid shelf on the floor of the Roasting Oven with a cold plain shelf on the second set of runners above. As a guide, for most packs allow 20-30 minutes – with many foods the immediate radiant heat of the Roasting Oven will cook them in as little as 75% of the time stated. Always check they are thoroughly cooked before use. Serve or transfer to finish off or keep hot in the Simmering Oven until required.

CONVENIENCE MEALS FOR CHILDREN

NUGGETS AND FISH FINGERS

Grill chicken nuggets and fish fingers in a tin on the first set of runners, turning occasionally. Home-made versions of these can also be made. Lightly dust the chicken or fish in some seasoned flour. Dip into beaten egg and milk and then in breadcrumbs. These cook better on a piece of Bake-O-Glide on a baking tray lower down in the oven.

OVEN CHIPS

Cook oven chips in a single layer in a tray on the floor of the Roasting Oven. For home-made oven chips, peel and slice into strips. Rinse well in cold running water until it runs clear. Dry thoroughly in several clean tea towels. Place in a bowl and add a little oil. Toss thoroughly so that they are all given a very thin coating. I prefer to add a little cayenne pepper to help improve the colour and also give a little heat. Spread out on Bake-O-Glide on baking trays and cook in the Roasting Oven. Use the floor of the oven and shake from time to time. Swap trays around if cooking more than one tray.

BAKED BEANS AND SPAGHETTI

Baked beans and spaghetti hoops heat through beautifully in an hour in a covered shallow dish on the floor of the Simmering Oven. If in a hurry, place in a shallow Pyrex dish on a grid shelf on the floor of the Roasting Oven.

RE-HEATING FOOD

With the Aga you can re-heat food instantly using the stored heat in and on the cooker. It is important that food is always re-heated really thoroughly, until it is piping hot. Only re-heat something once, so heat up what you will be able to use and leave the rest in the refrigerator for up to three days.
For most foods the Roasting Oven is the best place to re-heat food. Dense food are best sliced to ensure that heat penetration is effective.

If in doubt, cook in a container on the grid shelf on the floor of the Roasting Oven until heated through to the centre. If necessary, slide in a cold plain shelf to prevent browning too quickly.

SLICED MEAT AND POULTRY

Place slices in an ovenproof dish or use an Aga roasting tin. Add a little cold water so that the base of the container is barely covered and crimp tightly with foil. Place on the floor of the Roasting Oven for 7 minutes, until piping hot.

ROAST VEGETABLES AND TRIMMINGS

Place roast vegetables on Aga baking trays and re-heat until crisp on the floor of the Roasting Oven for 8-12 minutes. Left-over oven-baked trimmings such as stuffing can re-heat in the middle of the Roasting Oven for 15-20 minutes.

VEGETABLES

Place in the top of a collapsible steamer in a saucepan with hot water below. Cover and bring to the boil on the Boiling Plate. Transfer to the Simmering Plate for 3-5 minutes, until piping hot.

SOUPS, SAUCES AND GRAVY

With care, these can be started off on the Boiling Plate, stirring all the time until they are hot. Finish off with a few minutes on the Simmering Plate, or heat for the whole time there, covered, stirring occasionally.

STEWS AND CASSEROLES

Place the pan on the Simmering Plate and slowly heat through. Alternatively, place the pan on a grid shelf on the floor of the Roasting Oven. When hot, simmer for a few minutes on the Simmering Plate before using. Check that pieces of meat and poultry are piping hot. Cooked meat and poultry should never be re-heated using the Simmering Oven. Always use the Roasting Oven and do not re-heat more than once. The reason I do not recommend using the Simmering Oven alone for re-heating, is because it is difficult to determine if food has heated up fast enough to keep within recommended food safety re-heating parameters.

TAKE-AWAYS

If a take-away is not needed immediately, remove from any plastic bags and place the whole paper package in the Simmering Oven to keep hot for several hours until wanted. Don't forget to put plates to warm so they are piping hot when you are ready to serve your meal.

4. RECIPE CONVERSION TECHNIQUES

The first thing you notice when you start cooking on an Aga, is that the heat you want for any particular function is always instantly available. In most decades since its introduction over seventy years ago Aga owners have been regularly surveyed, asking what they most liked about their cooker. Without exception it has never been one particular part of the cooker that they liked best, despite the popularity of the legendary Simmering Oven, the rapid Boiling Plate or the fast Roasting Oven. 'Immediate readiness' has always come out top. The luxury of being able to bake just one potato properly at no expense, or being able to boil water so quickly at any time day or night, is what owners appreciate more than anything else. Instant heat is the other advantage that Aga owners could never again manage without. When converting a recipe for the Aga, no pre-heating is required.

In this section I examine a number of common recipe instructions and show that whatever is required may be easily undertaken with the Aga. Some are obvious techniques, while others may come as a surprise. You will soon be able to integrate them into your cooking and add others to make using your Aga as easy as possible.

FOUR STEPS TO GUARANTEE SUCCESS

1. SELECT THE CORRECT OVEN AND APPROPRIATE HEAT ZONE

Remember, to obtain the desired temperature and cooking conditions, control is provided by positioning and timing alone. You don't set the heat with an Aga: you find it. By selecting the correct position in the cooker the food will cook to perfection, with the cooker temperatures being automatically adjusted by the thermostat. Consult the What Cooks Where sections in chapter one and the Baking Conversion Matrix at the end of this chapter to decide where would be the best starting point for your recipe.

2. MONITOR THE COOKING PROCESS AS REQUIRED THROUGHOUT THE COOKING

Because you never need to be afraid of opening an oven door to see how cooking is progressing, it is fine to check on things early. I suggest you do this about 60-70 per cent of the way through the time suggested in the recipe. For most things cooking times are similar to those with conventional cookers, but with quite a few you have the advantage of faster cooking times.

3. NOTE THE POSITION WITHIN THE OVEN AND RATE OF COOKING AND BROWNING

Make a note of what you did, and the results you obtained. If you modified the conditions, such as by adding a cold plain shelf to slow any browning, note this for consideration in the future.

4. ADJUST YOUR TECHNIQUE NEXT TIME YOU USE THIS OR A SIMILAR RECIPE

You may want to fine-tune your technique next time you use this recipe:

Consider using a different shelf position for a slightly different rate of browning
Consider using a different hot oven in a 3 or 4 oven cooker
Consider using a cold plain shelf above for some or all of the cooking
Consider using the floor of the oven to speed up the heating up process
Consider moving food to a different oven during the cooking

TRANSLATING RECIPE INSTRUCTIONS

'FIRST SOFTEN THE ONIONS AND GARLIC...'

Where a savoury recipe begins with gently softening onions, apply the Aga principles and the rest is easy. Begin with the pan on the top of the cooker and heat some oil or butter. A mixture of the two helps prevent butter burning. Start on the Boiling Plate and add the onions, stirring to heat them quickly. If using garlic, add this a little later on to prevent any danger of it burning. Now transfer to the Simmering Plate and cover for a minute or two.

In most cases the pan can then be transferred to the Simmering Oven and left for 20-30 minutes to become tender. Return the pan to the top of the cooker and boil off any moisture that has collected. If browned onions are required transfer to the floor of the Roasting Oven. Check every few minutes and stir to prevent them burning. Alternatively they may be finished off on the top of the cooker if more careful supervision is required.

'BEGIN BY BROWNING THE MEAT...'

With recipes using minced meat, the gentle heat of the Simmering Plate is perfect for drawing out natural fat. Place the meat in a dry pan and allow the gentle heat to allow some of the fat to be released, stirring occasionally. Then transfer the pan to the Boiling Plate and stir constantly as the meat is browned. With a large quantity do this in batches to prevent the meat from steaming rather than browning. If using a pan without a plastic handle, or a cast aluminium pan which features a removable handle, the pan may be transferred to the floor of the Roasting Oven.

If diced meat is to be browned first toss lightly in seasoned flour, then brown in batches. Use a little hot oil in a pan on the Boiling Plate, taking care to avoid crowding the pan. After starting off on the top of the cooker, transfer the pan to the floor of the Roasting Oven and turn the meat every 5 minutes. Alternatively, heat some oil in a full size roasting tin on the floor of the Roasting Oven and when hot use this. Continue with the recipe, adding other ingredients and when all is simmering, transfer to the Simmering Oven to finish cooking.

'REDUCE THE HEAT AND SIMMER GENTLY...'

Many people's understanding of simmering is in fact slow boiling. Certainly, all rates of slow boiling are possible on the Simmering Plate. Simply partially offset the saucepan on the hot-plate until the desired rate of boiling is reached. However for textbook simmering, food should always be transferred to the Simmering Oven. This provides true simmering with the food cooking at the very gentlest rate possible.
The temperature here is comparable to when cooking on a hob with the liquid occasionally emitting just the merest blip on the surface of the food. The food will continue in this way without any supervision. For the gentle simmering of stocks, *see* the stock-making notes on page 32.

'START AT... AND TURN DOWN...'

The simple practice of positioning to determine the correct temperature, also applies when moving food from one oven to another. Once food has come to temperature in a hot oven, where a recipe instructs the oven to be turned down, simply move the food to a lower position, or to a cooler oven in the case of 3 and 4 oven cookers. In a 2 oven cooker the coolest place in the Roasting Oven is on the grid shelf on the floor of the oven – the home position. If a cooler setting than this is required, insert a cold plain shelf onto the second set of runners above. To prolong this period, replace the plain shelf with another cold one after 30 minutes.

'INCREASE THE HEAT AND REDUCE...'

To reduce a sauce, the Boiling Plate can be used for rapid boiling. If, however, this will take some time and the Roasting Oven isn't being used for other things, the pan may be transferred to the floor of the oven and left to reduce, steam being carried away by the oven vent. If a long time is permissible for the reducing process and the food is then to be cooked slowly in the Simmering Oven, do this without a lid and the liquid will also reduce at a much slower rate. This should not be done if this oven is required for cooking other foods at the same time which require an oven free from steam.

'BAKE IN A PRE-HEATED OVEN AT 200°C...'

'Bake in a pre-heated oven at 200°C (400°F) or Gas Mark 6 for 20 minutes. When golden brown and bubbling, reduce the oven to 180°C (350°F) or Gas Mark 4 for a further 20 minutes...'

When cooking layered dishes such as shepherd's or cottage pie as well as baked pasta and sauce combinations such as lasagne, it is easy for the dish to become over-cooked on the outside if cooked at too high a temperature. For this reason, some recipes call for the temperature to be reduced so that the top of the dish does not become over-browned while the heat penetrates to the centre of the dish during cooking. This can often be the case when baking a prepared deep dish after it has been stored uncooked in the refrigerator. In a 3 or 4 oven cooker the Baking Oven may be used and as it is at a lower temperature, the rate of cooking will be slower giving a chance for a thorough cook in the time it takes to brown. In a 2 oven cooker, bake on a grid shelf on the floor of the Roasting Oven and when it has browned attractively, slide in a cold plain shelf above so that little further browning occurs whilst the food cooks completely to the centre.

'ADD THE ALCOHOL, TILT THE PAN AND ALLOW TO IGNITE...'

Without the presence of a naked flame, obviously it is necessary to light the alcohol burning off with a match or lighter. Where a gas hob option is present, this may be used to light a taper.

'FRY SUCCESSIVE BATCHES IN TWO PANS OVER A MODERATE HEAT...'

Where a recipe calls for this kind of technique, for example to soften aubergine slices, instead lightly coat them with oil and place on baking trays. These can be cooked in the Roasting Oven on the floor and at the top of the oven. Turn after 5 minutes and after a further 5 minutes they may be cooled and used in a recipe as directed, e.g. Moussaka or Aubergine Parmesan.

'PRE-HEAT THE OVEN TO ITS HIGHEST SETTING...'

'Pre-heat the oven to its highest setting. Roast for 10 minutes per pound (450g) and then turn off the oven and leave the door closed for 40 minutes before removing to serve...'

This is a technique in a conventional cooker using a hot and then falling oven, typically suggested for the very best cuts of beef such as fillet. Sometimes a recipe will instruct you to brown the meat all over in a pan before roasting. The Aga Roasting

Oven operates at a temperature higher than that obtainable in a conventional cooker, so it is perfect for this technique. As with all roasting, make sure that the meat is at room temperature before starting, to ensure that the timings work correctly, so remove from the refrigerator for at least 30-40 minutes for a small joint, up to an hour for a large one. Roast for 10 minutes per lb (450g) as instructed, hanging the roasting tin from the lowest set of runners in the Roasting Oven, then remove and quickly wrap in foil and transfer to the coolest oven in your cooker to rest for the following adjusted times:

	2-5lb (900g-2.25kg)	**5¼lb (2.5kg) and larger**
Warming Oven	10 minutes per lb (450g)	15 minutes per lb (450g)
Simmering Oven	8 minutes per lb (450g)	10 minutes per lb (450g)

Return to the Roasting Oven for 5-10 minutes to make the joint crisp again and then carve immediately. This will give a beautiful result with a crisper exterior and an excellent moist rare centre. Deglaze the juices left in the roasting tin when making a simple gravy or sauce.

'TURN UP THE GRILL TO ITS HIGHEST SETTING TO BROWN THE TOP...'

Gratins

Where a recipe instructs the oven to be turned up to brown a topping, place a grid shelf on the highest set of runners in the Roasting Oven that will allow the dish to be placed as high up as possible – with the food almost touching the roof of the oven. For recipes such as Lancashire hotpot or other dishes covered with slices of potato or mashed potato, brush with a little milk, in which you have dissolved half a teaspoon of salt, to encourage golden browning.

Meringue Toppings

For meringue-topped desserts, place on the grid shelf on the third set of runners in the Roasting Oven for only 2-3 minutes – but watch carefully. Then transfer to the Simmering Oven for 15-25 minutes to dry out the meringue a little if required. Most recipes suggest aiming for a soft, marshmallow centre and a crisp top with the peaks an attractive golden brown. *See* the Meringues recipe on page 136.

Sugar Glazes

Sugar toppings need to be browned right at the top of the Roasting Oven. As with all cookers, it is best to select an ovenproof dish which will just accommodate the mixture so that it comes to within $^1/_4$ inch (5mm) of the top of the dish. Watch carefully so it doesn't burn.

Crème Brûlées

Of all the methods suggested for Crème Brûlées, I think the following gives the easiest and most professional finish. The result is a crisp layer of caramel that you can make in the thickness that you prefer. It is also far quicker than resorting to a blow-lamp.

It is possible to make excellent crèmes brûlées on an Aga. I prefer making a large one, but individual ones are another option. Because they are so rich, I recommend making the custard over a fruit compote, either home-made or bought. Placed in the base of the mould they make a perfect foil for the silky set cream. For a lighter, low-fat variation, mix equal quantities of low-fat vanilla yoghurt with thick low-fat Greek yoghurt in place of the custard. It doesn't have the same silky texture of the authentic set custard, but is a good low-fat version for a family dessert. Here is a basic recipe that is easy and reliable as I know some people maintain that it isn't possible to make this with an Aga.

$^1/_2$ oz (15g) soft butter
6 egg yolks
6 oz caster sugar
1$^1/_2$ pts (850ml) single cream
1 tsp vanilla extract
6 tablespoons water
6 oz (175g) granulated sugar

Prepare a 7 x 1$^1/_2$ inch (18 x 4cm) circular shallow ovenproof dish by rubbing the butter around the sides and add the cold compote, if using. In a large bowl whisk the egg yolks with the caster sugar until very smooth and pale. Rinse out a heavy-based pan with cold water and then add the cream and bring to scalding point on the Boiling Plate. Pour over the egg mixture, whisking all the time. Pass the mixture through a sieve into the dish and place in a half size roasting tin. Pour boiling water into the tin coming halfway up the side of the dish. Add a slice of lemon to the water to prevent discolouring the tin if it is plain aluminium.

Cook on the grid shelf on the floor of the Roasting Oven for 10-15 minutes, until starting to set. Carefully transfer the whole assembly to the middle of the Simmering Oven for 45-60 minutes until completely set (it will set firmer once it is chilled). Remove the dish and leave in a cool place for 45 minutes before covering and refrigerating.

To make the caramel, place the water and sugar into a heavy-based pan and leave on the Simmering Plate until the sugar dissolves. When this has happened, transfer to the Boiling Plate and boil hard until the mixture starts to resemble the colour of runny honey. Pour slowly and carefully over the custard. Allow to set in the refrigerator and serve the same day. Take care not to splash the caramel as it is very hot. To clean the pan boil up some water to dissolve the hardened caramel.

'PLACE IN A PRE-HEATED OVEN AT GAS MARK 1...'

'Place in a pre-heated oven at Gas Mark 1 (140°C, 275°F) and after 10 minutes, reduce the oven to Gas Mark $^1/_4$ (110°C, 225°F). After an hour, turn off and leave in the oven overnight...'

This technique is sometimes suggested for cooking meringues and a pavlova. Too high an oven temperature can cause meringue mixtures to weep, and that is why this gentle method is sometimes advocated. The gentle heat found in the Aga Warming and Simmering Ovens is perfect for all types of meringue mixtures, and they may be cooked perfectly in both these ovens, taking a shorter time in the Simmering Oven. To prevent a pavlova over-cooking and losing its moist marshmallow centre, remove from the oven after 1-1$^1/_2$ hours. To dry meringues out thoroughly, allow 1$^1/_2$-2 hours. If necessary, remove from the oven after this period and turn them upside down and return to their parchment. Place the baking tray on a chef's pad on the Simmering Plate lid to continue to dry out gently.

'USE A SIMMER MAT OR HEAT-DIFFUSING PAD...'

Artificial aids such as mats and heat-diffusing pads are unnecessary and do not need to be resorted to. Their use would also waste heat so they should not be used.

The temperate heat of the Simmering Plate is perfect for gently making most sauces. A roux will cook here without any danger of burning and milk or stock for a sauce can be gently heated. If preparing ahead of time, liquid ingredients can be pre-heated in the Simmering Oven for half an hour beforehand. If you haven't pre-heated the liquid, draw a cooked roux to the side of a pan and add some cold liquid, and place this part of the pan over the Simmering Plate. When hot, whisk into the roux and then gradually add the rest of the liquid and cook the sauce to a smooth consistency. If you are in a hurry, with care you can use the Boiling Plate to incorporate a liquid when making a sauce, but it is essential to keep whisking thoroughly all the time the pan is on this hotplate. Alternatively, the all-in-one method can also be used on this hotplate, starting with all the ingredients cold, gently whisking all the time. Once thickened, continue to cook the sauce for a few minutes or as long as the recipe directs, either on the Simmering Plate or transferred to the Simmering Oven for slightly longer.

Emulsion sauces

The area of the enamelled top plate in front of and between the two closed lids is perfect for making, and keeping hot, delicate sauces such as Hollandaise and Béarnaise.

AGA OVEN STANDARDS

STOCK-MAKING

The gentle heat of the Simmering Oven gives excellent clear stocks, which often don't need clarifying for normal use. The attention of constant skimming is also done away with because the heating is so exact. Many cookery schools recommend the use of an Aga for making stock when one is available. For example, at Leith's School of Food & Wine, they independently give this recommendation of the Aga Simmering Oven in their students' notes:

'At least 3, and up to 8 hours over the gentlest flame, or in the bottom oven (Simmering Oven) of an Aga, is ample cooking time. In the Aga, skimming is unnecessary – as the liquid hardly moves there is no danger of fat being bubbled into the stock, and it can be lifted off the top when cold.'
Leith's Chef School

Everyday stock is really easy. Place a chicken carcass in a pan and cover with cold water and bring to the boil. Simmer for 5 minutes on the Simmering Plate. Then remove from the heat and add a cup of cold water. This will encourage any impurities to rise to the surface for easy skimming – a nylon tea-strainer is best here. Now add a clean unpeeled and halved onion, some roughly chopped carrot, together with a stick of celery if available and a few peppercorns, a bay leaf and some parsley stalks. Bring back to the boil and cover and transfer to the Simmering Oven for 3 hours. Cool, strain and refrigerate. Fat will solidify on the surface for easy removal. This freezes well.

It is worth making a batch of really concentrated chicken stock occasionally. Ask your butcher for lots of raw chicken necks and carcasses or buy some cheap chicken wings and really pack a saucepan full. Follow the method above and you will make delicious chicken stock that will turn to jelly when cold and which will transform home-made soups, sauces and casseroles.

Beef and veal stock may be made by first browning the bones in the Roasting Oven if wished. Vegetable and fish stocks require much shorter cooking times but follow the above method.

It is important in the interests of food safety that when making stock it is cooled quickly after it is removed from the cooker. Aim to have it cool enough for transferring to the refrigerator or freezer within 2 hours. To achieve this realistically, place the pan in the sink and surround with cold water. Stir the stock occasionally to speed up the process. This technique is particularly important when making large quantities. Always aim to cool cooked liquids as quickly as possible after cooking.

BREAD-MAKING

With the radiant heat from the Roasting Oven, baking bread at home is really easy. You certainly don't have to make your own bread if you have an Aga, but if you want to, it is the easiest cooker in the world to do this. I use my KitchenAid mixer with its dough hook and it takes only a few minutes' work, with several periods of proving which will happily proceed without your supervision. By all means use one of the excellent bread mixes that are now available, but they come at a price. Flour by the bag or sack is less than half the price. Once you have settled on a favourite recipe, find volume measures in your kitchen which you can use to save having to weigh anything.
I have an aluminium pint measure in my flour bag, and I know that to make my usual two 2 lb loaves, I need one and a half measures of flour. This takes one sachet of easy-blend yeast and the other ingredients are a two teaspoons of sea salt and a drizzle of olive oil. This needs 2 mugs of water using a certain mug, so I use one of cold water and one of water from a boiled kettle to achieve the warm temperature required for yeast mixtures. This goes into the mixer and then everything else bar the half measure of flour goes on top. I mix for a minute and then leave it to go spongy. When it has doubled in size, I switch on the machine again and add the remaining flour until the mixture has been kneaded well so it is well stretched and silky. I then hand finish the dough and work it into two equal loaves. These are dropped into the tins and left next to the Aga in a large oiled thick plastic bag kept for the purpose to prove beautifully. An hour or so later they are fully risen and I carefully transfer them to the oven and add an ice cube to the floor to generate steam.
I bake them on a grid shelf on the floor of the Roasting Oven. I set the timer for 35 minutes and that's about it. Sometimes I ring the changes by adding a large sliced onion to the mixture that has softened in a little butter in the Simmering Oven to transform one of the loaves into delicious onion bread if I am serving soup for lunch. Olive, sun-dried tomato and herb variations also all work well but for delicious walnut bread I use a special recipe. Although I do use that and other recipes from time to time, this is my 'daily bread' and it is easy enough to build into my normal routine.
I use a 50:50 mixture of white and wholemeal flour most of the time, all white flour occasionally for rolls, and sometimes equal quantities of white, wholemeal and multigrain.

STEAMED PUDDINGS

Until I started to cook on an Aga, I was reluctant to make steamed puddings for the simple fact that they normally need to be attended to for several hours to prevent them boiling dry. Kettles have to be boiled for regular topping up and the kitchen can soon resemble a sauna. This tiresome attention and mess is dispensed with in the Aga. The principle is to prepare your favourite recipe, using a sponge mixture or suet crust, and add the raw sweet or savoury filling. Cover with the usual discs of parchment and foil etc., pleating the final coverings to allow for expansion. Place in a pan and pour hot water around to come half-way up the pudding basin. If using an aluminium pan, add a slice of lemon to prevent discolouration. Bring to the boil on the Boiling Plate and then transfer to the Simmering Plate for 30 minutes. This initial slow boiling period is important for sponges so that they immediately start to rise. In the case of meat fillings, these also need to start getting hot initially to cook in the normal timings. Transfer the pan, water and pudding to the Simmering Oven for the remaining normal cooking time. For sponges allow $2^1/_2$-3 hours; for sweet suet puddings allow about 3 hours, up to 4 if containing fruit. Meat suet puddings take 6 hours and Christmas puddings turn deliciously dark if cooked for 8 or more hours, or even overnight (to re-heat your Christmas pudding before serving, *see* the Christmas section, pages 111-119).
The Aga Cake Baker is excellent for steamed puddings as the internal carrier can be used to remove the cooked pudding easily and safely. With its metal handles it can also be used on the floor of the Roasting Oven for the preliminary 30 minutes' boiling period, transferring it to the Simmering Oven to finish cooking.

SMOKING FOOD

The Aga Roasting Oven is perfect for hot roasting meat and fish. Purchase smoker chips or very fine barbecue chips – I like oakwood or hickory best. Other chippings including applewood and whisky-soaked oak are also available. Try anglers' shops or barbecue specialists if you have difficulty finding them.

Choose a suitable ovenproof container that you can also easily cover reasonably tightly with a lid or makeshift lid. I have used round and oval Aga cast iron casseroles and also Aga half size roasting tins. The latter work well as you can use the grill rack in the low position and a second roasting tin inverted as a lid, using a water and flour paste as a sealing gasket. Another option is the Aga Cake Baker if you have one. This has a tight-fitting lid and a built-in carrier.

Whichever utensil or strong-based tin you use the method is the same: a base part is heated for 10 minutes on the floor of the Roasting Oven until it is very hot. In the meantime, prepare your meat or fish. 6 oz (175g) main course size fish fillets are good (cooking time 15 minutes) as are whole trout (best to smoke for 15 minutes, then return and finish open baking for up to 10 minutes), or try small duck or pheasant breasts (cooking time 20-25 minutes). Lightly oil your grill rack, if using a roasting tin, or other cooking trivet. If using a cake baker I would place a circular rack inside an old 8 inch (20cm) sponge tin to save mess. Round and oval casseroles need a similar rack arrangement. Place your food on the oiled rack leaving plenty of space around each piece.

Transfer the hot base to the Simmering Plate and add your dry wood chips. As a guide, use 2 tablespoons. They must not be pre-soaked in water as when using on a barbecue. I would recommend lowering them in on a simple tray made of two thicknesses of foil to save making a mess. Now add the rack with food and cover with your chosen lid. If using two roasting tins, carefully apply the flour and water paste to the rim of the top tin, before squeezing this down on top of the other tin. Transfer your covered assembly to the floor of the Roasting Oven for the required cooking time. If using roasting tins, it is easier to slide them in lengthways so that the flour paste joint does not foul the runners. Traces of smoke from the cooking assembly are of course safely vented away from the oven due to the oven ventilation system. When the cooking time has elapsed, use thick Aga gauntlets to carry the assembly to an outside work surface. Uncover the smoker and the surplus smoke will quickly disperse in the open air. Opening it up in the kitchen is not recommended. Check for doneness, and if necessary return to the Roasting Oven for a few more minutes if not cooked to your liking.

Another variation to try is smoking with a mixture of tea and sugar placed in a foil parcel and added in the above manner. This method is far more satisfactory than home-made assemblies used on the Boiling Plate, as they invariably fill the room with smoke and the cook ends up as kippered as the food!

VEGETABLES AND PULSES

As well as steaming vegetables in the normal Aga way, Ratatouille is also very easily made. After the onion and green peppers have been sautéed until just starting to soften, the garlic and remaining ingredients can be added and the whole mixture brought to a simmer and transferred to the Simmering Oven for cooking over several hours.

For pulses, after an overnight soak in cold water, these may be drained, rinsed and then covered with fresh water. Bring to the boil on the Boiling Plate and then continue to cook on the Simmering Plate for 15 minutes before transferring to the Simmering Oven to cook in the normal times. To prevent toughness, do not add any salt until the pulses are tender.

SOUS VIDE COOKERY

There are certain food writers who are proponents of ultra-slow cooking, or the sous vide method. This is a technique that involves poaching ingredients in sealed plastic pouches which are then placed in water kept at a set low temperature. These are usually vacuum-packed – 'sous vide' is French for 'under vacuum' – for an extended period of time, often at much lower temperatures than normal. This is employed in certain commercial kitchens and some restaurants. Correctly carried out this can give excellent results. Some cookbooks are now recommending improvising this method at home using zip-lock plastic bags. Sous vide foods are also starting to become available in some supermarkets.

Normally, with very few exceptions, all food placed to cook in the Simmering Oven must be thoroughly heated elsewhere on the cooker as the set gentle heat of this oven is only sufficient to continue cooking food that is already hot. If converting a recipe for using these low temperature methods in the Aga Simmering Oven, it is vital that a thermometer is used when bringing the cooking liquid to the required cooking temperature, to ensure that a minimum temperature of 60°C (140°F) is held before transferring the food to the Simmering Oven. Providing this temperature is reached and held, the food will continue to cook at or very slightly above this temperature in the Simmering Oven which will ensure safe results.

YOGHURT, CHEESE AND JUNKET

Make your own Aga yoghurt using the normal method. First rinse out a milk pan with cold water and add 2 pints (1.2litres) of semi-skimmed or full cream milk. Place on the Simmering Plate and bring to scalding point – the surface should just shimmer. Remove and allow to cool slightly, then whisk in 3 oz (75g) of dried milk powder. When at blood heat (37°C/98°F), stir in 2 fl oz (60ml) of live yoghurt. Leave undisturbed on a trivet or folded tea towel just on the edge of the top plate or Warming Plate for 4-12 hours or overnight until set. Chill before serving.

Make your own curd and cottage cheese by adding 2 teaspoons of rennet to milk that has been scalded on the Simmering Plate as above and then cooled to blood heat (37°C/98°F). Leave the bowl on a trivet on the Simmering Plate lid to set. Use an Aga chef's pad or thick cloth to protect the lid. When the curds and whey separate, strain overnight in a sieve lined with a paper coffee filter in the refrigerator.

For a delicious junket, warm a pint of fresh semi-skimmed or full cream milk to blood heat (37°C / 98°F) on the Simmering Plate. Stir in 2 tablespoons of sugar with 1 teaspoon of rennet essence and set aside until completely set. Place on a cork mat on the top plate and leave undisturbed for some hours. This is perfect for serving with summer fruits as a change from Panna Cotta.

SLOW COOKING TECHNIQUES

'Cook it low, cook it slow' cooking offers many advantages. Food tastes better and there is no danger of things burning or boiling over.'
The slower the cooking the better the result' is so true. The food tastes better because the flavours have had time to develop and concentrate while shrinkage is reduced. Apart from roasting premium cuts, with beef I invariably use the slow roasting method at home. Lamb I would cook no other way as the results are so succulent and the juices make the most wonderfully concentrated addition to the perfect gravy.

When meat in stews and casseroles is cooked at a lower temperature and for a longer period, the gentle heat enables the connective tissues and meat to become very tender indeed. Cheaper cuts with a lot of flavour can therefore be used to great advantage and yield meltingly tender results with virtually no care or attention in their moist, slow cooking. This method will beautifully tenderise delicious but tough cuts such as shin of beef, oxtail, neck of lamb, pie veal and boiling fowl, all with succulent results. Regional favourites such as Irish stew and Lancashire hot-pot take on a whole new meaning when they are slowly cooked in the Aga. Because the rate of cooking is so slow, timings are relatively imprecise – it is hard to over-cook things and casseroles are quite undemanding. This is a great advantage for those with busy lives and the routines of today. Slow-cooking in the Aga Simmering Oven can greatly lighten your work load and it is something that is well worth exploring.

Less evaporation occurs when cooking at low temperatures, so when using a new conventional recipe, typically measure the liquid quantity recommended, and use enough to just cover the food. This often means that you can hold back about 10%. Keep this in the refrigerator to add to the cooked dish if it needs it; often the consistency will be perfect without. As well as making stock that will transform your cooking generally, delicious soups can be made in larger batches. These can then be frozen in pint yoghurt pots for easy lunches. I routinely make a double batch when cooking a casserole or stew and freeze half for an easy meal the following month. In this way you can always have a couple of wholesome meals that are quick to prepare without becoming totally enslaved by the full 'always cook for the freezer' mantra. Casseroles and stews keep their flavour particularly well. To keep the best texture when serving a re-heated frozen dish, replace the flour in the recipe with cornflour, or leave it out completely and thicken using beurre manié when finally reheating. Mix together equal quantities of soft butter and plain flour to a paste and drop pellets of this into the hot liquid. Allow to simmer for 5 minutes until the flour has thoroughly cooked and thickened the liquid.

The Simmering Oven is a bain-marie in itself and with many recipes, after starting off in a hot water bath in the Roasting Oven for 30 minutes, the food container can be transferred in its water bath to finish cooking gently. With some recipes it can be found that containers tightly wrapped in foil can even safely continue cooking on their own in the Simmering Oven. Delightfully smooth or coarse pâtés, terrines and galantines work really well and I think an enamelled cast iron rectangular mould is a great investment – it is smart enough for the table for family meals. These can be quickly lined with bacon, the mixture made in moments in a food processor and then packed in and set to cook. Custards will cook to a silky conclusion without over-cooking and becoming grainy. Velvet-like cheesecakes can be cooked for many hours with a perfectly set top and with no cracks appearing.

MEAT, POULTRY AND GAME STEW AND CASSEROLES

There are two methods that may be used. I was always taught to brown meat at the beginning of a recipe for two reasons. Firstly, it is thought to improve the flavour and secondly it should also give colour to the dish. I still generally use the browning method but on occasion use the all-in-one technique and it certainly has its place. One of the best steak and kidney pies I ever tasted was in an award-winning Gastropub and I was so impressed that I met up with the chef in question. A little sheepishly he confided that the mixture was brought to the barest simmer in vegetable stock and left to cook on virtually a pilot light for six hours before being finally thickened. Maybe it was the Guinness they added that worked the magic.

It is important that meat is thoroughly defrosted if it has been frozen. Similarly if using frozen vegetables these must also be treated in the same way. Slice or chop the onion and other vegetables. These actually take longer to cook than meat and poultry as they cook at the higher temperatures so avoid using large pieces as they are less likely to be tender even after many hours' cooking. In busy households it may be easier to prepare everything the night before so that the assembly is a quick affair before the meal is put into the oven to cook for many hours. I have found that when slow cooking stews and casseroles it is best to be quite assertive when seasoning at the beginning, but to leave adjusting the salt until the dish is cooked.

Browning Method

Heat a little oil or fat and start to soften the onions, garlic and vegetables. I usually use a large Aga cast iron casserole as the tall sides contain splashes and one pot saves on washing up. A non-stick pan also works well, as virtually no fat is needed. Aim for the onions to start to colour at least until they are golden then remove and reserve. Add the floured meat and brown in batches on all sides, avoiding over-crowding the pan. A little more oil or fat may be needed but at the end, drain off any surplus oil or fat. If freezing part or all of the dish, omit the flour and consider thickening later in the recipe. Add the chosen stock and liquid to the pan and use a wooden spatula to deglaze the base of the pan. Add the vegetables and then the meat and mix well, adding herbs and seasoning – but go easy on the salt. Cover and bring to temperature on the Simmering Plate. Ensure that all the vegetables are submerged in the cooking liquid; the meat should be mostly covered. When thoroughly heated through, transfer to the grid shelf on the floor of the Simmering Oven for at least 2-3 hours. When cooked, if necessary thicken with beurre manié as described above or use another thickening medium. Taste and correct the seasoning.

All-in-One Method

Complete the assembly in the order as above, without browning the vegetables or meat. Skinless chicken and most white stews invariably dispense with the browning process.

Prepare Ahead Method

A stew or casserole may be prepared ahead by either of the above methods, and then kept in the refrigerator overnight. The liquid ingredients must be kept separate and heated first on their own the following morning. If using the browning method, it is important that the vegetables and the meat are allowed to cool completely before storing in the refrigerator. Hot or warm food should never be placed in a domestic refrigerator. First thing the following morning, take the casserole ingredients from the refrigerator and leave to come to room temperature for up to an hour. Heat the liquid ingredients gently in the casserole on the Simmering Plate and when just about to simmer, add the onions and vegetables, partially offsetting the pan if necessary. When it has returned to almost a simmer, add the meat and continue with the method.

TOPPINGS

With shallow casseroles, once the dish is ready, a topping can be added. Here are my favourites:

Make a simple savoury scone mixture and stamp out small rounds to arrange around the edge of the casserole. Bake in the middle of the Roasting Oven until just light and golden.

Make a savoury crumble topping using the normal proportions of butter to flour, but add a teaspoon of mustard and some Gruyère and parmesan cheese. Pipe sieved mashed potato over the meat and brown at the very top of the Roasting Oven.

Toast one side only of some oval slices of French bread, turn them upside down and rub with garlic and then pile on grated cheese. Place around a casserole or soup and brown at the very top of the Roasting Oven.

KEEP SAFE

It is important not to assemble a complete recipe in a casserole to refrigerate overnight, to then heat straight from the refrigerator the following morning. There would be a danger of incomplete heating which could cause cooking at too low a temperature with the consequence of a food safety risk.

As with all cooked foods, once served, cool quickly before storing in the refrigerator and freezer. The Simmering Oven is not generally suitable for safely re-heating cooked foods. Hotter parts of the cooker should always be used to make sure that the food is quickly and thoroughly heated until piping hot.

AGA BAKING CONVERSION MATRIX

The following oven baking positioning calculator will enable you to work out how to cook with total confidence any conventional baking recipe in your Aga.

2 OVEN AGA BAKING GUIDE

Absolutely any cake can be cooked in a 2 oven Aga when it is at full temperature, using the techniques already explained and the methods and positionings listed below. The cold plain shelf is the primary method of providing a moderate baking temperature, using the Shielding Principle (*see* page 20). If the oven has been previously cooled slightly by other cooking, you can take advantage of this, so when having a cooking session plan to cook cakes after other things. When having a full baking session, plan to succession bake using a slowly falling oven – start with baking bread and pastry requiring a hot oven, then cook sponge cakes and biscuits needing a more moderate temperature, finishing with any deeper cakes which require a very moderate oven. In some cases this will mean that when you are well into a baking session a cold plain shelf will not be required in the normal way – it will be obvious to you as you are cooking if this is the case.

Always use the cold plain shelf when instructed, inserting it cold onto the second set of runners down at the same time the cake is put into the oven to bake. For cooking times longer than 30 minutes, if necessary replace the cold plain shelf with another to maintain a moderate oven below the shelf and a hot oven above.

3 OVEN AGA BAKING GUIDE

The Baking Oven in the 3 oven Aga works in the same way as that found in the 4 oven model. A useful extra feature is that when using all of the ovens and hotplates together for many hours, i.e. under a heavy load, the Baking Oven will, over time, slowly start to increase in temperature. If baking under these conditions, a cold plain shelf above cakes and biscuits may be required to cut off top heat if necessary. This effect generally only normally occurs when cooking large roast meals, where an extra hot oven is most welcome.

Small Cakes and Fairy Cakes These require a short cooking time in a hot oven	
2 Oven Aga	Bake for 8-10 minutes, turning once. Use an Aga roasting tin on the lowest set of runners in the Roasting Oven. Alternatively, use a bun tin on the grid shelf on the floor of the oven.
3 or 4 Oven Aga	Bake for 8-10 minutes, turning once, at the top of the Baking Oven.

Swiss Rolls These require a short cooking time in a hot oven.	
2 Oven Aga	Bake for 7-8 minutes in the coolest position of the Roasting Oven. This is on the grid shelf on the floor of the oven. They do not require shielding from top heat with a cold plain shelf as the cooking time is so short.
3 or 4 Oven Aga	Bake for 7-8 minutes in the coolest position of the Roasting Oven. This is on the grid shelf on the floor of the oven. They do not require shielding from top heat with a cold plain shelf as the cooking time is so short.

Scones These require a moderate to hot oven. The middle of the oven is used.	
2 Oven Aga	Bake on the third set of runners in the Roasting Oven for 8-10 minutes, until a pale golden colour.
3 or 4 Oven Aga	Bake on the third set of runners in the Roasting Oven for 8-10 minutes, until a pale golden colour.

Choux Pastry
Eclairs and profiteroles, etc. require a hot oven.

2 Oven Aga	Bake on the lowest set of runners in the Roasting Oven for about 15-20 minutes.
3 or 4 Oven Aga	Bake on the lowest set of runners in the Roasting Oven for about 15-20 minutes.

Tray Bakes, Victoria Sandwiches, Gingerbreads, Parkins and Biscuits
These require a medium cooking time in a moderate oven.

2 Oven Aga	Bake in the Roasting Oven, hanging an Aga roasting tin on the lowest set of runners or place the cake tins on the grid shelf on the floor of the oven. Place a cold plain shelf on the second set of runners above for the whole of the cooking time. Use the lowest set of runners for baking biscuits with the cold plain shelf above. If batch baking biscuits, later batches may not require a cold plain shelf.
3 or 4 Oven Aga	Bake in the Baking Oven, which is of a moderate temperature. Hang an Aga roasting tin on the lowest set of runners or place the cake tins on the grid shelf on the floor of the oven for the required cooking time. Biscuits may be cooked on the fourth set of runners in the Baking Oven. No cold plain shelf should be required, but can always be used if necessary.

Shortbread
This needs a very moderate baking to achieve a perfect sablé finish.

2 Oven Aga	Bake in the Roasting Oven, hanging the roasting tin on the lowest set of runners, or a baking tray on a grid shelf on the floor of the oven. Slide a cold plain shelf on the second set of runners above. Bake for 15-20 minutes, turning once. When a very pale golden colour at the edges, transfer to the third set or runners in the Simmering Oven for 30-40 minutes to finish cooking to an even pale colour.
3 or 4 Oven Aga	Bake in the Baking Oven. Hang an Aga roasting tin on the fourth set of runners or place the tins on the grid shelf on the floor of the oven. Bake only to an even pale colour, turning once.

Large Deep Cakes requiring over 45 minutes' cooking time
Deep cakes, such as almond, cherry, Madeira and light and rich fruit cakes, require a longer cooking time at a moderate temperature.

2 Oven Aga	Bake 6, 7 and 8 inch (15, 18 and 20cm) deep round cakes in a pre-heated Aga Cake Baker on the floor of the Roasting Oven. Bake for 1-1¼ hours, or up to 1½ if the oven is a little cooler than usual. **Moderate Baking Method if no Cake Baker is available** Place a large grill rack in a full size Aga roasting tin in the low position. Place the cake on this and slide onto the lowest set of runners in the Roasting Oven. Slide a cold plain shelf above onto the lowest set of runners possible. Bake for 20 minutes and then replace with another cold plain shelf. If a full size Aga baking tray is available, use this sandwiched with a cold plain shelf for longer protection. Alternative, it is possible to transfer the cake to the Simmering Oven to finish cooking, once it has set and is an even colour. To do this, transfer the hot plain shelf to the middle of the Simmering Oven. Transfer the cake to this hot shelf and continue to cook for 1-1½ hours.

3 or 4 Oven Aga	Bake in the Baking Oven, placing the cake tins on the grid shelf on the floor of the oven for the required cooking time. No cold plain shelf should normally be required.

Fruit Loaves and Tea Breads

These require a longer cooking time at a moderate temperature.

2 Oven Aga	Bake two 1 lb (450g) loaf tins placing one inside a pre-heated Aga Cake Baker on a grid shelf on the floor of the Roasting Oven, with the second tin in front of the Cake Baker towards the front of the oven. The Cake Baker will absorb sufficient heat to prevent the unprotected cake becoming over-cooked. Protect with foil towards the end of cooking if absolutely necessary.
3 or 4 Oven Aga	Bake in the Baking Oven, placing the loaf tins on the grid shelf on the floor of the oven for the required cooking time. No cold plain shelf should normally be required.

Fruit Pies and Tarts

In all cookers, these are best in a hot oven to cook the pastry and then at a lower temperature to finish cooking the filling if necessary.

2 Oven Aga	Bake on the floor of the oven, or on the grid shelf on the floor of the Roasting Oven. When the pastry is nicely browned transfer to the Simmering Oven for 20-45 minutes for the filling to continue to cook until it is tender.
3 or 4 Oven Aga	Bake on the floor of the Roasting Oven, or on the grid shelf on the floor of the Roasting Oven. When the pastry is nicely browned transfer to the Simmering Oven for 20-45 minutes for the filling to continue to cook until it is tender.

Flans and Custard Tarts
In all cookers, these may be baked using raw pastry as baking blind is not necessary. The bottom heat from the floor of the oven will cook the pastry crisply before the custard has a chance to make it soggy. The custard will set in the time it takes for the pastry to become perfectly cooked.

2 Oven Aga	Bake on the floor of the oven in the Roasting Oven for 20-35 minutes, until the pastry is crisp and the filling set and golden.
3 or 4 Oven Aga	Bake on the floor of the oven in the Roasting Oven for 20-35 minutes, until the pastry is crisp and the filling set and golden.

Rich Fruit Cake, Slow Method
This is a further technique where the cake is cooked slowly in the Simmering Oven of all models. It is perfect for cooking large cakes for weddings and other celebrations. Follow your favourite recipe and method for the correct amount of mixture for the size and shape of tin specified in the recipe. A small cake can take anything from 4-8 hours, depending on the age of the cooker, a large cake 6-15 hours. When you initially try this technique, I recommend you do this during the day so you can keep an eye on things. The gentle heat of the Simmering Oven will cook the cake to perfection with exceptionally moist results.

2 or 3 Oven Aga	Bake on the grid shelf on the floor of the Simmering Oven.
4 Oven Aga	Bake on the floor of the Simmering Oven, or if making in a full size Aga roasting tin, hang on the single middle runners.

Cooking Times

Depending on the age of your Aga, the cooking time will vary – older cookers have slower Simmering Ovens. Once you have cooked one cake by this method you will be able to determine suitable cooking times easily using the following formulae. As an initial guide, with a modern Aga, allow 30 minutes per inch (2.5cm) for a round cake and 40 minutes per inch (2.5cm) for square cakes. With older cookers featuring slower Simmering Ovens, allow an hour per inch (2.5cm) for a round cake and 1¼ hours per inch (2.5cm) for square cakes. The first time you try this method, start checking for doneness several hours ahead of time – an inserted skewer should come out clean when the cake is cooked.

If a shorter cooking time is desired, the cake may be started off in a hotter oven first:

2 Oven Aga	Bake on a grid shelf on the floor of the Roasting Oven with a cold plain shelf on the third set of runners above for 25-30 minutes, before transferring to the Simmering Oven.
3 or 4 Oven Aga	Bake on the lowest set of runners in the Baking Oven for 30-40 minutes, before transferring to the Simmering Oven.

A few final pointers

Some very rich fruit cake recipes call for quite a large quantity of fruit juice, ale or other alcohol to be used to soak the fruit and add to the cake mixture. Baking in the non-drying heat of the Aga Simmering Oven can cause rich fruit cakes to take too long to cook using the slow method. This can produce more of a 'pudding' effect than a normal cake finish. To adapt such recipes, add only a quarter of the alcohol specified in the recipe and use the remainder to 'feed' the underside of the finished cooked cake.

Many rich fruit cake recipes require several layers of extra protection to be used as well as the normal lining of the tin. Because of the 'kind to food' heat of the Aga ovens, only a single lining using of Bake-O-Glide or baking parchment is required even when cooking the richest fruit cakes. Extra layers of cartridge paper, brown paper or newspaper are not necessary and can be dispensed with. These are only required for these types of cakes to protect the cake from burning in conventional cookers.

From experience over many years of talking to and observing Aga owners in their own homes, I have discovered that one of the most important things to be grasped is to have complete confidence in the power and capacity of the Simmering Oven. It is like having another pair of hands in the kitchen. Early Aga adverts even described it 'as good as having a kitchen maid'! Many people have admitted to me that, even after attending demonstrations, they still have only been using their Simmering Oven for warming plates, because they didn't believe it was hot enough to cook food. Resolve to use it correctly and you will never look back. The under-use of the Simmering Oven and over-use of the Simmering Plate, often with saucepans with poor bases, are invariably the two main causes of losing heat.

5. AGA ENTERTAINING

Whenever I cook without an Aga, such as when I am helping to entertain in the homes of my friends, the thing I miss most is the way that an Aga can keep everything hot so easily, without anything spoiling. The set temperatures of the Simmering and Warming Ovens can never over-heat, and their ability to keep food in good condition is far superior to the conditions found in electric hot cupboards and serving trolleys. You can use your best dinner service and even cook the vegetables in the tureens themselves, safe in the knowledge that they will come to no harm. There never seems to be any last minute panic with an Aga, either.

A seemingly never-ending supply of hot plates, serving dishes and pre-prepared sauces can easily be produced with very few things actually needing to be cooked right at the last minute. Even notoriously temperamental courses such as soufflés can be served with confidence, because the radiant heat of the ovens means that mixtures are guaranteed to rise spectacularly. These can be prepared ahead of time, using the popular twice-cooked method, and sweet mixtures can even be made and frozen raw, to be baked in the hot Roasting Oven for 20 minutes before serving. With a service this smooth, your guests could well assume you have staff!

CATERING FOR PARTIES

The beauty of the Aga is that when cooking for parties you really do effortlessly enter the stress-free world of Aga entertaining. As well as giving faithful service for normal everyday cooking, the Aga always rises to every occasion which means that you actually start to enjoy having your friends for dinner. It is the large capacity of the ovens which allows you to cook a lot of food at the same time. You can also start cooking well beforehand so that when your guests are about to arrive there is less to finish off. This is true whether you are throwing a full-blown dinner party or simply filling the house with friends for an informal supper. Because the food can be kept beautifully without deterioration it really doesn't matter if your guests are running late. You can simply sit back and relax, safe in the knowledge that the cooker quite literally has everything under control.

To simplify matters, always aim to have some of your courses completely finished before your guests arrive. My preferred combination is to serve hot canapés, then a cold starter, followed by usually a hot main course. In the summer it is sometimes a good idea to have some part of the main course hot. For example, to go with a cold main course and salads, perhaps serve hot new potatoes with butter and chives. This is especially a good idea when eating al fresco when the weather is questionable. Desserts can obviously be made and decorated beforehand and left in a cool room ready for serving later. Pre-prepare the coffee tray with petits fours etc., so that only milk and hot water need to be added at the last minute.

I receive a lot of letters and e-mails from owners keen to learn how to cook basic foods for large numbers, with many questions on different cooking timings, etc. Therefore, as well as starting with more sophisticated techniques I have included a section covering this subject. The examples given should help you in applying the same principles to other favourite recipes.

RUNNING OUT OF HEAT

There is absolutely no need to turn up your Aga before cooking a large meal. The heat reserves are enormous and if you use the cooker correctly you will have plenty left over even after cooking a great deal of food. Incidentally, once you are cooking, advancing the control 'to give it a boost' is pointless anyway – as soon as you start to use some of the stored heat, the heat source will have quickly increased to its highest setting. Twiddling the control knob further will not make it go any higher. I know some owners insist on running their Aga a little higher than usual on occasion, and that is a matter of personal choice, just as in some houses the Aga is turned down a little during the hottest weeks of the year. Cooking times in both cases will be altered. From observation, when owners resort to turning up their cooker, this usually means they are trying to compensate for incorrect use of the cooker as a whole.

ESSENTIAL EQUIPMENT

Full size Aga baking trays and roasting tins are invaluable when entertaining and cooking for large numbers. Saucepans with the correct bases are absolutely essential if cooking large quantities of food. Aga preserving pans and stockpots are therefore extremely useful. If you are cooking a lot of food ready to serve at a specific time, always allow longer in your timeplan – it is always easier to slow cooking down by moving food or by taking cooked dishes out of the cooker. For Cooking for Numbers, *see* page 119.

CANAPES FOR BUSY PEOPLE

When you have an Aga, your guests always seem to think that you will automatically be serving interesting nibbles. I think they must read in between the lines of adverts in magazines. If the mere thought of piping bags causes your heart to sink, fear not. There are plenty of delicious canapés that you can quickly produce which are really very easy and ideal for entertaining. Many can even be prepared raw and then open-frozen and kept in bags in the freezer. When friends drop in, whether two or twenty, instead of reaching for the crisps, you can quickly serve stylish nibbles to go with drinks by placing them on a tray and baking for seven minutes in the Roasting Oven. Everyone will think you are the best host in the world. Following are five simple favourites for you to try that can also be made in large numbers using baking trays. If possible, try to always offer a selection of at least two contrasting canapés.

EASY CROSTINI

This is more of an assembly method than a recipe. You can ring the changes endlessly with different ingredients. I usually use toppings and cheeses that are on promotion. Here are the ones I have been using most recently. Ask me in six months' time and the list will have changed again. Use your imagination when shopping at the cheese counter. Your basic ingredients are part-baked baguettes or petits pains and softened butter.

Bake the bread on a grid shelf in the middle of the Roasting Oven for 7 minutes until cooked and lightly coloured. When cool, slice on the diagonal into $^1/_4$ inch (5mm) thick slices. Butter both sides lightly and then give the top of each a small coating of a savoury paste such as pesto, tapénade or sun-dried tomato paste. Then add a suitable topping – here are some suggestions to get you started:

- **A drained 'Peppadew' pepper, mozzarella pearl and basil leaf**
- **A cornet of Parma ham with cream cheese inside**
- **A slither of Brie with a small wedge of fresh ripe pear**
- **A slice of prosciutto torn into pieces with diced pear and crème fraîche**
- **A thin piece of sliced or crumbled cheese with a pinch of paprika**

At this point these may be open frozen, then packed into plastic bags or boxes until ready for use. Place on a baking tray lined with Bake-O-Glide, and cook on the floor of the Aga Roasting Oven for 5-8 minutes until golden and crisp. Keep an eye on them, as they cook quickly, and serve immediately. The heat from the floor of the Roasting Oven is used to ensure that bases are deliciously crisp. If necessary, use the floor of the Baking Oven for another tray, but if you need to cook several trays, use the Roasting Oven, swapping the trays around during cooking.

EASY BLINIS

Traditionally these are made using a yeast-raised batter, but this simpler type require hardly any time to make and as they are made smaller than usual most people won't notice the difference. These freeze very well if wrapped tightly in foil and can be re-heated on trays in the oven after defrosting. Use the standard drop scone mixture from page 137, but use half buckwheat flour and half self-raising. Make small 1 inch-sized pancakes and serve topped with a little soured cream and caviar or crème fraîche with smoked salmon strips topped with a feather of dill.

EASY CROUSTADES

Cut out circles of thin white bread using a biscuit cutter and roll thinly. Brush with melted butter and press each one down into a mini muffin tin with a second tin on top to hold them down. Bake low down in the Roasting Oven for 6 minutes until crisp. Fill with a savoury mixture of your choice such as a little smooth pâté, pairing this with a little sweet contrast such as mango chutney or honey.

EASY MINI QUICHES

Purchase several dozen ready-made one inch (2.5cm) mini pastry cases. Fill with a little of your chosen savoury filling and pour in the savoury flan mixture from page 58 adding a small pinch of finely grated cheese. Bake these on a plain shelf using Bake-O-Glide using the lowest set of runners in the Roasting Oven for 10-12 minutes, until lightly set and just coloured. After cooling, these may be re-heated just before serving on the floor of this oven for 3-4 minutes just before serving warm.

EASY MINI PALMIERS

Take a pack of ready rolled puff pastry – the all-butter type for preference. Roll a little thinner still and cut into two long thin rectangles. Spread each very sparingly with a little ready-made English mustard. Scatter over some grated Parmesan and Gruyère cheese and plenty of freshly ground black pepper. Taking each piece in turn, fold the two long ends into the middle, brush with a little water and then repeat. Press down well and wrap in clingfilm. At this point they may be frozen, as the pastry being safe to re-freeze. When required, take from the refrigerator or allow to defrost. With a sharp knife cut into 1/4 inch (5mm) slices and place on Bake-O-Glide on a plain shelf. Flatten each slightly, then bake on the second set of runners in the Roasting Oven for 6-10 minutes until golden brown, turning once. Variations are endless: try using Patum Peperium, tomato purée, tapénade or red or green pesto.

EASY MINI SUNDAY LUNCHES

Prepare Yorkshire pudding batter using the recipe on page 134. Use a cast iron grill pan to grill some fillet steak medium-rare and leave it to rest for 10 minutes on a warmed plate. Using a sharp knife, cut into thin slithers. Whip a little double cream until thick and fold in some bought horseradish sauce, a little salt and freshly ground black pepper and a squeeze of lemon juice. Heat a little oil in the bases of two mini muffin tins on a grid shelf on the second set of runners in the Roasting Oven for 5 minutes. Pull out the shelf and remove the first tin to the Simmering Plate. Pull the second tin to the front of the shelf and pour in batter to half-fill each hole, and then push to the back of the shelf. Repeat with the first tin. Allow 8-12 minutes for them to cook and then cool a little on the top of the Aga. Whilst still warm and crisp, fill each with a dash of the horseradish cream, topped with a slither of steak and a sprig of parsley or coriander. These can be assembled ahead of time and then re-heated for 5 minutes before serving hot.

GET AHEAD PREPARATIONS

When cooking a lot of food for a large number of people, the Aga makes short shrift of cooking lots of vegetables and trimmings for a roast meal. If serving roast beef, I always make Yorkshire puddings first thing in the morning: mini, medium or several large ones using the half size roasting tins. Cook until perfectly risen and golden. Allow to cool and then keep covered with a clean cloth in a cool place until just about to serve your meal. Return the Yorkshire puddings to the oven for 3-5 minutes and they will re-heat perfectly, ready for serving. For my 'oven-buster' recipe, *see* page 132. Roast potatoes, parsnips and other vegetables can easily be two-thirds roasted the day before your big meal and kept in a cool place and then finally finished off in the oven on the day. Similarly, for large Christmas meals, up to 4 large Aga baking trays will fit in the oven at one time, so large quantities of baby chipolatas, stuffing balls, bacon rolls, etc. can also be accommodated at the same time. Careful planning is obviously important to ensure that everything is cooked and nothing forgotten.

GET AHEAD VEGETABLES

PEEL AHEAD

When cooking for roast meals such as Sunday lunch and during the holidays, take the easy way with preparing most of your vegetables ahead of time. Here I share some of the tricks of the trade that will make it all seem so easy. Fill your vegetable tureens with raw vegetables as you prepare them so that you can gauge the perfect quantity for the best possible perfection. Potatoes and root vegetables can be pre-prepared ahead of time with no loss in quality. For most green vegetables, however, it is best not to prepare them too far ahead of the actual cooking – do the final cutting just before use, but remember a lot of pre-trimming can be done in advance. It is even possible to cook some green vegetables ahead of time (see below) if you wish, however for the best results I prefer to cook most green vegetables right at the last minute. As the Aga is taking care of everything else, this is easy to do under your close supervision to make sure that they are cooked perfectly. Potatoes can be peeled and kept covered with water in the refrigerator, with carrots and other root vegetables in polythene bags.

PARBOIL AHEAD

Potatoes and parsnips can be parboiled a day ahead if you wish. For potatoes, try to use a good floury variety such as Desirée, King Edward or Maris Piper. Place even-sized pieces in cold salted water and bring to the boil in a large saucepan on the Boiling Plate. Adjust the heat as necessary and continue cooking gently on the top of the cooker until the potatoes are just starting to soften. Start testing with a skewer after about 8 minutes. Drain well for 5 minutes, until the steam subsides, then shake well in the colander or dry pan, to roughen each potato lightly. When cool, refrigerate in plastic bags and bring to room temperature for an hour next to the Aga, or on a cloth on the top plate before roasting. If cooking from cold they will take a little longer than if freshly par-boiled. Incidentally, you may question whether you could use the Simmering Oven for this process. This is certainly possible, but it is best to stop boiling at just the right moment to achieve the correctly softened surface of potato for perfect roasting. Remember, when supervision is required for some reason, never be afraid to use the top of the Aga. If you practise, you can in fact find the correct time for par-boiling potatoes, but the timing varies so much between varieties, which is why I recommend using this method instead.

ROAST AHEAD

Potatoes can be roasted ahead the day before your meal; cook as below until they just start to colour, they will take about three-quarter the normal time – approximately 30-40 minutes. Drain off the fat, cool and then keep covered in the refrigerator until the following day. Bring back to room temperature for several hours before finishing off on the floor of the roasting oven for 20-30 minutes. As with the normal method, swap several trays around.

Parsnips and other root vegetables can be similarly roasted in advance and then finished off for 20-30 minutes in the middle of the Roasting Oven before serving.

BLANCH AHEAD

To cook some green vegetables ahead of time, use the following professional method for perfect results. This works best with beans, broccoli, mange tout, Brussels sprouts and most other green vegetables. Boil in fast-boiling salted water on the Boiling Plate for up to 5-7minutes until just cooked, depending on their thickness. Watch carefully and test. Drain and immediately refresh by plunging into a bowl of well iced water for five minutes. This will arrest the cooking and set their bright green colour. Drain again and refrigerate for up to three days. When required, re-heat in a pan on the Simmering Plate for a few minutes with a small amount of water, adding a knob of butter once the water has evaporated, just before serving.

PERFECT VEGETABLES EVERY TIME

Because so much of your cooking can be left to cook in the Aga without requiring endless supervision, you will find that you are left free to concentrate on the parts of a meal which, on a conventional cooker in the rush of things, can get over-cooked. This also means that you can easily attempt something requiring a little last-minute supervision, such as quickly stir-fried or wilted spinach, cooked in a wok with some simple seasoning.

PERFECT ROAST POTATOES

For superlative roast potatoes that will be the envy of experts, seek out some Graisse d'Oie, the best goose fat from France. If this is not available, a mixture of half vegetable shortening and half olive oil works brilliantly. Heat your chosen fat or oil in a baking tray or roasting tin on the floor of the

Roasting Oven until good and hot. Add the par-boiled potatoes and turn them so that a flat surface of each is facing downwards. Now baste the rest of the surfaces with the hot fat. I like to use a heat-proof pastry brush which makes this a quick task, but you can also baste with a spoon and turn them in the fat if you prefer. The brush method means you can use a lot less fat. I also prefer the results of roasting potatoes directly in the tin. Alternatively, Bake-O-Glide may be used – virtually fat-free roast potatoes are therefore possible if required. Ideally, roast potatoes should always be cooked on the floor of the Roasting Oven. If cooking several trays, rotate them around periodically so that they all enjoy a spell crisping on the floor of the oven.

PERFECT ROAST ROOT VEGETABLES

Oven-roasted root vegetables have a concentrated flavour with a gently sweetened effect. Par-boil as for potatoes, but not enough for the surfaces to become roughened. Mixtures of two work well both for colour and flavour. Experiment with squash, pumpkin and sweet potato, pairing with carrot, parsnip swede and turnip. When roasting parsnips, a little honey or syrup added near the end of the cooking gives an attractive glaze. Alternatively, dredge with a little grated Parmesan and parsley.

PERFECT ROAST MEDITERRANEAN VEGETABLES

Oven-roasted Mediterranean vegetables are delicious and extremely versatile. Cut up your choice of several peppers, red onion, courgettes and aubergine into similar sizes and place in an Aga roasting tin. Drizzle with olive oil and seasoning and toss well. Half-crushed cloves of garlic and herbs such as rosemary are ideal additions – leave to marinate, if possible. Roast on the floor of the Roasting Oven, shaking the contents every ten minutes or so until they are just tender.

PERFECT WINTER VEGETABLES

Cook all root vegetables using the Aga Oven steaming method (*see* page 31). As well as serving in batons, sliced or diced, with a little butter and parsley if liked, they are also delicious mashed, creamed or puréed. Carrot with swede, squash or sweet potato makes an easy dish with great colour and flavour. Add a little of the cooking liquid with some crème fraîche and season with black pepper and a little freshly grated nutmeg. This also keeps hot well in the Warming or Simmering Oven and re-heats beautifully.

PERFECT POTATOES

New potatoes can be cooked with fresh mint using the Aga steaming method (see page 31). Serve with a little melted butter and a few chopped chives. Similarly, cooking old potatoes using this method ensures that even specimens which would normally turn to a mush cook through properly. Serve with a little butter and freshly chopped parsley, or turn into creamy mashed potato. Because they do not fall apart in any cooking water the result is dry and floury, ready to accept your choice of butter, hot milk or cream. Taste and season carefully before serving. Alternatively, use my 'no-peel' method below.

PERFECT GREEN VEGETABLES

Prepare them with a sharp knife and have ready a large broad-based pan and colander. Boil a kettle first and keep hot ready for pouring into the pan for rapid boiling at the last minute on the Boiling Plate. With the pan fully on the Boiling Plate, drop your prepared vegetables into lots of rapidly-boiling salted water. The huge reserves of heat will immediately return the water back to the boil so that a vibrant green colour is guaranteed. Partially offset the pan if necessary and cook until tender. I use a timer to prevent any danger of over-cooking, but testing with a skewer is the ultimate check – seven minutes is plenty, if you cut green vegetables appropriately. Avoid cooking anything thicker than 1/2 inch (5mm). For example, with broccoli, cut the trimmed stalks thinly on the diagonal and drop these into the boiling water. Cook for three minutes before adding the florets so that they are all perfectly cooked at the same time. Drain and serve immediately.

Alternatively, green vegetables can be steamed. Place a collapsible steamer in the base of a saucepan. Pour in boiling water to almost come up to the base of the steamer. Bring to the boil on the Boiling Plate and add the green vegetables. Keep the water boiling hard to generate a good supply of steam and then partially offset the pan or move to the Simmering Plate. Steam with the lid half on the pan to contain the steam whilst still allowing excess to escape, along with the sulphurous compounds released from the vegetables. Once one pan has been started off, others may follow; begin by cooking first those green vegetables with the longest cooking times.

AGA SERVING TRICKS

I am endlessly experimenting with different techniques to discover and rediscover new ways of producing delicious food as easily as possible with the Aga. Anything that can help keep mess and washing up to a minimum at the last minute is always welcome. In this section I share some of my favourite ways to save on work when entertaining, from not having to peel potatoes to being able to wash up saucepans before your guests have arrived. When I am entertaining, I like to finish what I have been doing in the kitchen with a dishwasher full and put to work, all the surfaces and table clear with only a few things left out. At the most I might have perhaps two green vegetables near the Aga for cooking at the last minute, and a few trays of canapés waiting to place in the oven when my guests are due. I can leave everything else safely stowed in the Aga where it can come to no harm. This means I am free to put on a CD, open some wine to breathe and sit and relax with a short break before my guests arrive. This way I can actually enjoy my own party.

NO-PEEL CREAMED POTATOES

Here is my technique for producing delicious mashed and creamed potatoes using the Aga so that you will never have to peel potatoes again. Choose potatoes that are all roughly the same size and that, when halved, will fit into a potato ricer. Scrub well and cut each in half. Bring to the boil in salted water on the Boiling Plate and simmer for 3-5 minutes. Drain and transfer to the Simmering Oven for 20-40 minutes, until tender. Place each potato cut-side down in a potato ricer and use it like a giant garlic press – the cooked potato will be pushed through the ricer and each time the skin will be left behind to be discarded. Continue with the remaining potatoes working quickly so that they remain hot. Return the mash to the saucepan and keep the mixture on one side. Add milk, butter or cream to the exposed base of the pan and season well. Place the pan so that the liquids only are heating on the Simmering Plate, and when hot, beat or whisk into the potato until it is all light and fluffy. Taste and re-adjust seasoning if necessary. If you haven't already tried them, creamed potato with another ingredient makes interesting variations; use half and half – potato and turnip or swede mixtures are delicious, also celeriac or sweet potato. Butter, spring onions or chives are other additions worth experimenting with.

COOKING IN VEGETABLE TUREENS

Once you have mastered the Aga vegetable steaming method (*see* page 31), try my development of this technique, where the vegetables can finish cooking in their actual serving dishes. Pre-heat your empty vegetable tureens in the Simmering Oven for an hour beforehand, using dinner plates as temporary lids. Par-boil root vegetables and potatoes using the normal Aga method and then drain and transfer quickly to the hot tureens in the Simmering Oven. Here they can finish cooking – simply allow a little longer than usual, about an extra five minutes. This allows you to wash and put away saucepans before your guests arrive, minimising the washing up required by hand at the end of your meal. Heat other empty tureens stacked inside themselves in the Warming or Simmering

Ovens ready to receive other vegetables such as roast potatoes and lightly cooked green vegetables. Warm the lids on the top of the Aga with any sauce boats so that all the handles remain cool enough to lift.

VEGETABLE PLATTERS

Flat ovenproof china serving platters can be used with the blanch and refresh technique (*see* page 104) for serving a selection of vegetables when entertaining. Each of the vegetables can be prepared ahead of time and then re-heated perfectly when required. Either use a large platter that fills the floor of the Roasting Oven or use several smaller dishes for individual portions or a medium dish for two servings. This works for all steam-presented vegetables but not for roast potatoes or parsnips which can be added afterwards, if required. Vegetable purées are also possible but not creamed or mashed potato, as the starch would stick to the dish during re-heating.

To pre-prepare your vegetables, boil each type separately in batches in fast-boiling salted water on the Boiling Plate for just a few minutes until just tender. Different varieties will take slightly different cooking times. Once cooked, immediately remove them (using a wire blanching basket makes this an easy task) and plunge them into iced water, as described on page 106. Pat dry and arrange on the serving platters. Brush with a little melted butter, season well and add two tablespoons of water per person being served. Cover with foil and crimp it around the edge very tightly. This will now keep in the refrigerator for up to 48 hours before being used. Remove to room temperature an hour before needed and then re-heat on the floor of the Roasting Oven for 12-15 minutes – just long enough for the dish and the vegetables to become piping hot. Watch for wisps of steam escaping from the foil as an indication the vegetables are ready and do not become overcooked.

ROLL-OVER GRAVY

To save the stress of last minute gravy-making, use my Aga roll-over method for making delicious home-made gravy with a full depth of flavour to complement your roasts. It totally liberates you from being tied to the cooker at the last minute as you guests arrive. Next time you have a roast, pour the roasting juices into a small bowl and allow to cool. Serve with a sauce prepared ahead of time. After the meal, carefully save the solidified pellet of fat from the top of the roasting juices, which will be full of flavour, and wrap in foil. Transfer the jellied roasting juices to a plastic container. Place the roasting tin on the Simmering Plate and add a little stock or hot water to deglaze the tin. Stir, using a flat wooden spatula. When all the debris has dissolved, pour this stock into a third container. Freeze the fat, jelly and stock and use next time you serve roasted meat or poultry. Follow my master gravy recipe method below. In this way you can make a really good-flavoured gravy from scratch an hour or so before the meal is ready to serve, which will echo the flavour of the roast itself. More importantly, you can take trouble over checking that it is just the right consistency and colour and that the flavour and seasoning are perfectly balanced. This can then keep hot in a covered pan in the Simmering Oven to be served with the new roast. The fat and juices from the new roast can then be saved ready for the next one. I try to keep in my freezer beef, lamb, pork, chicken, turkey and game gravy packs ready for use with the method below.

PERFECT GRAVY EVERY TIME

Most people have their own favourite way to make gravy. All methods can be followed on the Aga, but I prefer the roll-over method described above. Once you have a supply of different home-made gravy kits in the freezer it greatly simplifies the final stages of cooking a roast meal, freeing you to linger with your family and friends. A lot of people at demonstrations tell me they want to know how to make perfect gravy from scratch, so here is my simple guide to help you. I will describe the saucepan method first, which I prefer because it is quicker, but the same principles can be used with the second method where the gravy is made in the roasting tin.

Where possible always use some fat from the meat you will be serving, as fat carries flavour and your gravy will then have a strong back note of the relevant flavour to complement the main dish. One of the reasons I suggest roasting a few onions and root vegetables in the tin with a roast is that during cooking the vegetable sugars will brown naturally to help ensure a rich colour and flavour for your gravy.

For every pint of thin gravy wanted, make a roux in an Aga saucepan with 1 oz (25g) of fat taken from the roasting tin and 1 oz (25g) plain flour. For a thicker gravy use 2 oz (50g) of each per pint. Cook for a couple of minutes, adding a little extra fat if at all dry. Carefully pour off all the remaining fat and reserve for cooking, but leave all the congealed cooking juices in the roasting tin. Add enough good-flavoured stock or reserved vegetable water to the roasting tin to cover the base and place on the floor of the Roasting Oven or on the Simmering Plate for a few minutes. Use a flat-ended wooden spatula to encourage all the concentrated juices and sediment to dissolve into the liquid. Pour this gradually onto the roux and whisk in thoroughly. Repeat the deglazing process as required until the roasting tin is rendered clean and all the juices have been whisked into the roux. Add more stock to thin down to your preferred consistency.

At this point you can add a little fruit jelly to complement your meat, e.g. use a little redcurrant or mint with lamb, venison and game, crab apple or apple with pork, etc. A proportion of red or white wine can also be used instead of stock. Simmer for several minutes to cook out the flour taste and for it to finish thickening. Then taste and carefully adjust the seasoning, adding salt and freshly ground black pepper. If liked, add a little dry sherry and a little cream. Check the seasoning again. When transferring the roast from resting to its serving platter, add to the gravy the juices that will have accumulated. Keep hot in the Warming or Simmering Ovens and strain into the previously warmed gravy boats before serving.

If you prefer to make gravy in an Aga roasting tin, remember that these should never be placed over the direct heat of the Boiling Plate as over time this will cause them to distort. They should only be used on the Simmering Plate or on the floor of the Roasting Oven. Follow your usual method, removing excess fat from the tin and making a roux by adding an equal quantity of flour. Stir this in and allow to cook for several minutes. Then gradually whisk in your chosen liquids – vegetable water, stock, a little wine, etc. Simmer the finished gravy for several minutes to reduce and thicken. The cast aluminium baking dish with its heavy base may be used for making gravy on the Boiling Plate if desired.

RELAXED SAUCE-MAKING AHEAD OF TIME

Custard and sauces can all be made ahead of time and kept hot in covered pans or Pyrex jugs covered with cling film in the Warming or Simmering Ovens. With white sauces, it is best to add any flavouring, cheese, etc. just before using. Leave washed herbs on a board with a sharp knife for chopping just before your guests are due and add to the hot sauce just before use. Bread sauce can similarly be made early without deteriorating.

HOT PLATES AND SERVING DISHES FOR CROWDS

If you are serving a meal for more than 20 people using a 4 oven Aga and have a Warming Plate, there is a useful trick to know when heating plates. Fill the Warming Oven several hours ahead of time with the dinner plates. Towards the end of your cooking, transfer the thoroughly heated plates to sit in two piles on top of the Warming Plate. Cover these with several clean towels and they will remain piping hot for a very long time. This frees up the Warming Oven for keeping a large quantity of already cooked food hot.

If you have a lot of plates and serving dishes to heat, and your Aga is full of food, fill your dishwasher with all your china and put it on a heat only (drying) cycle, or on the shortest wash option. Do a dummy run to time the length of the programme, and then you can set the dishwasher off at just the right time to result in hot dry dishes exactly when required. This tip never fails to impress onlookers. It is especially useful if you are cooking for more than ten people with a two or three oven Aga – the Simmering Oven can then be used exclusively for cooking and keeping food hot.

THE FAMOUS AGA CHRISTMAS

At Christmas an Aga excels itself, producing the most delicious roast meals possible. The large capacity of the Aga ovens is perfect for all the cooking over the holiday period. With Christmas cooking it is important to bear in mind that most people like a reasonably traditional menu. Each year decide on making one new thing for a change to serve as a surprise, be it interesting home-made canapés, a tangy sorbet to serve between courses, or easy Aga chocolate fudge – prepare it in secret and hide it away. This will be the part of the meal your guests will remember most, talk about, and cause them to think you are an absolute star in the kitchen. However, it is not generally a good idea to jazz every dish up – by all means introduce a few new ideas, but keep the basics reassuringly familiar. Concentrate on cooking the vegetables well and work to a simple written-out time plan so that nothing is forgotten. This way *you* will enjoy everything too! With careful planning the work on Christmas Day itself can be kept to a minimum so that you can enjoy opening presents and spending time with family and friends. Enlist help the day before for peeling vegetables and preparing the trimmings. Children love to be involved with helping to lay the table, making festive place cards, etc. Don't forget that Bucks Fizz makes Christmas Day more enjoyable for the cook!

GET AHEAD AT CHRISTMAS

Pick up your fruit and vegetable order the same time as you collect the bird from the butcher and don't forget to buy some lardons (fat bacon) to cover the breast while cooking. Remove the giblets and use all but the liver to make giblet stock in the Simmering Oven ready for the turkey gravy. The liver with some chicken or duck livers can make a delicious easy Christmas pâté. Potatoes and parsnips can be peeled and stored under water in the refrigerator. Carrots can be peeled and left in a plastic bag and Brussels sprouts can be trimmed, removing any discoloured leaves, and then stored in the refrigerator in a polythene bag containing a little water. Also peel chestnuts for stuffing or for serving with Brussels sprouts as this is a time consuming job. Make your stuffing and allow to become cold before storing in the refrigerator ready for using it to stuff the neck just before you are ready to roast the bird. Make bread and cranberry sauces and prepare bacon rolls and other trimmings ahead of time and keep in the refrigerator.

ALL THE TRIMMINGS

As well as the usual Get Ahead advice for vegetables (*see* pages 103-104), for Christmas I strongly suggest investing in some full size Aga baking trays for cooking large quantities of roast vegetables and trimmings. Allow plenty of time if cooking more than two trays of roast potatoes, giving each a turn on the floor of the Roasting Oven. Four full size Aga baking trays can fit in one go in the Roasting Oven for all your trimmings. Grill bacon rolls at the top of the Roasting Oven with other trimmings in the middle of the oven. If cooking a large quantity of chipolatas or bacon rolls, thread them onto pairs of long skewers. These can then be turned in one go when needed so that they cook evenly with the minimum of fuss. Place bread sauce in the Simmering Oven to re-heat when you put plates and serving dishes, etc. to warm in the Warming Oven early in the day.

CHRISTMAS DESSERTS

To re-heat your Christmas pudding on Christmas Day, you don't need to steam it in the conventional way. Wrap the china, plastic or foil pudding basin tightly in foil and simply place in the Simmering Oven all morning, next to the turkey if necessary. Over several hours it will slowly and safely heat through, ready for serving piping hot at the end of your meal. To flambé your Christmas pudding with spectacularly sustained flames, unmould onto a really hot serving plate. Then warm equal quantities of cheap brandy and vodka in a pan on the Simmering Plate before pouring over and lighting. The secret ingredient is the vodka which will sustain the flames spectacularly for several minutes. Custard and brandy sauce can all be made ahead of time and kept hot in covered pans or in Pyrex jugs covered with cling film in the Warming or Simmering Ovens. Place a plate of mini mince pies on a plate in the Simmering Oven for 15 minutes before serving. This will produce pies with a warm filling that won't burn any tongues and spoil the Christmas festivities.

THE PERFECT AGA TURKEY

DEFROSTING FROZEN BIRDS

Weight	Thawing Time
5lb / 2.25kg	20 hours
10lb / 4.5kg	22-24 hours
15lb / 6.75kg	24-28 hours
20lb / 9kg	40-48 hours
25lb / 11.25kg	48+ hours

If you decide to have a frozen bird it is essential that you allow it to defrost slowly for the correct length of time.

Thaw the turkey in the coolest room – below 16°C (60°F). Remove any packaging first and check regularly. Once defrosted (no ice crystals remaining in the cavity and with the legs quite flexible), store covered, low down in the refrigerator at a temperature of no more than 5°C (40°F). Remove the bag of giblets as soon as they become loose during defrosting. If you are short of refrigerator space, a car boot in December may be cold enough for the safe storage of an uncooked bird once you have taken delivery of it on Christmas Eve. Alternatively, use an unheated room or animal-proof outhouse.

GIBLETS

Remove the bag of giblets from inside a fresh bird as soon as you take delivery of it. Whether from a fresh or frozen bird, use these to make your own giblet stock ready for making the gravy – it really is worth it and it's so easy in the Aga Simmering Oven.

STUFFING

Rinse the inside of the bird with cold water and pat dry with paper towels. Season the insides of both cavities with salt and pepper and a generous amount of butter. In the interests of food safety, with a turkey it is recommended to stuff the neck end only. In the body cavity place a quartered peeled onion and halved lemon together with a stick of celery, a few batons of carrot with some sprigs of fresh parsley and thyme which will pervade the bird with aromatic flavour. By all means prepare the stuffing ahead of time, and then refrigerate or freeze it, but do not stuff the bird until just before you are ready to roast it, using stuffing that is at room temperature. Additional stuffing can be cooked in a separate dish, and given several bastings of turkey roasting juices as it cooks. It is not recommended to truss a bird as leaving it untrussed allows free circulation of heat to all parts of the bird. Use bathroom scales covered with clingfilm to weigh the stuffed bird if necessary. Remember to weigh the bird after stuffing to calculate the correct cooking time.

WISHBONE REMOVAL

A tip to make the carving more elegant is to remove the wishbone before cooking. This will vastly facilitate carving the breast giving you lovely even slices. Either ask your butcher to do this for you in advance before you collect your bird, or do it yourself using a small sharp paring knife and cut carefully to avoid piercing the skin. Loosen the skin at the neck end and ease your fingers up between the breast and the skin. Cut the wishbone at the base end near the wing joints first. Cut up along the bone to remove it from the flesh and loosen at the top, twisting to remove. You might like to consider asking your butcher to remove the leg tendons before roasting.

ROAST FROM ROOM TEMPERATURE

It is vital that the bird is not roasted straight from the refrigerator. Roasting times allow for cooking a bird from room temperature, i.e. one that has been taken out of the refrigerator at least an hour before cooking.

TENTING WITH FOIL AND BASTING

When you are roasting a turkey or goose, remember that you are cooking two different types of meat – the delicate light breast meat, which must not be allowed to dry out, and the darker leg meat which takes longer to cook. Aim to make a roomy tent of foil over the bird to protect the breast from over-browning and also use foil to protect the legs if they start to brown too quickly. With an Aga, basting is only needed very occasionally during periods in the Roasting and Baking Ovens. If necessary, remove the foil for the last 30 minutes to crisp the skin.

Decide which roasting method best fits in with you and your family and calculate the total cooking time carefully. Make a list of your complete menu and plan a simple timetable to ensure that nothing is forgotten and that everything arrives at the table hot and in perfect condition. Note the times to start different vegetables in descending order. This takes the stress out of The Big Day.

AGA TURKEY ROASTING TIMES

In the interest of food safety it is important that the internal temperature of raw poultry should rise from room temperature to 60°C (140°F) within four hours at the start of the cooking. With the slow method this is particularly important, which is why I recommend an initial period in the hot roasting oven. All cooking times are approximate.

WHOLE TURKEY AND TURKEY CROWN (WHOLE BIRD WITH LEGS REMOVED)

Fast Method (2, 3 and 4 oven Aga cookers)
Rub liberally with butter. Place in the Aga roasting tin, on a grill rack if liked. Hang from the lowest set of runners in the roasting oven for one hour until nicely browned, then tent loosely with foil. These are the ***total*** fast method roasting times:

8-12 lbs	3.6-5.4kg	1¾-2 hours
12-16 lbs	5.4-7.25kg	2-2½ hours
16-20 lbs	7.25-9.0kg	2½-3 hours
20-24 lbs	9.0-10.8kg	3-3½ hours
24-28 lbs	10.8-12.6kg	3½-4 hours

Medium Method (3 and 4 oven Aga cookers only)
Rub liberally with butter. Place in the Aga roasting tin, on a grill rack if liked. Hang from the lowest set of runners in the roasting oven for up to one hour until nicely browned, then tent loosely with foil. After the first hour in the Roasting Oven, transfer the turkey to the Baking Oven to finish cooking, for the following ***additional*** times.

8-12 lbs	3.6-5.4kg	1½-2½ hours
12-16 lbs	5.4-7.25kg	2½-3½ hours
16-20 lbs	7.25-9.0kg	3½-4½ hours
20-24 lbs	9.0-10.8kg	4½-5½ hours
24-28 lbs	10.8-12.6kg	5½-6½ hours

Slow Method (2, 3 and 4 oven Aga cookers)
Rub liberally with butter. Place in the Aga roasting tin without a grill rack. Roast on the floor of the roasting oven for up to one hour and as soon as it starts to brown, tent loosely with foil. After the first hour in the roasting oven, transfer the turkey to the simmering oven to finish cooking, for the following ***additional*** times.

8-12 lbs	3.6-5.4kg	3-5 hours
12-16 lbs	5.4-7.25kg	5-7½ hours
16-20 lbs	7.25-9.0kg	7½-10 hours
20-24 lbs	9.0-10.8kg	10-12½ hours
24-28 lbs	10.8-12.6kg	12½-15 hours

BONED AND ROLLED TURKEY ROASTS

Ballottine of Turkey
Boned turkey with loin of pork and stuffing
Boned and Rolled Turkey
White and dark meat
Butterfly Breast Turkey
2 breasts of fillet meat
Cockatrice or Russian Doll Roast
Several birds of varying sizes, one inside another
Saddle Of Turkey
2 breasts of fillet meat, boned with wings inserted
Stuffed Turkey
With a ham, pheasant breasts or ox tongue and forcemeat stuffing
Swan Roast
A pheasant inside a chicken inside a duck inside a turkey with stuffing between the layers
Turducken
A chicken inside a duck inside a turkey with sausage meat stuffing. A 15-20 lb (6.75-9.0kg) turkey with a 5-6 lb (2.25-2.7kg) duckling and a 3-4 lb (1.3-1.82kg) chicken is the largest that may be safely managed.

Unless expressly instructed otherwise in a specific Aga recipe, these are all best roasted in the Aga Roasting or Baking Ovens by the fast or medium methods. Have the roasting tin on the lowest set of runners. Because they are so dense, it is essential to ensure that they are thoroughly cooked right to the centre. The use of a meat thermometer is strongly recommended. The slow method is not suitable for these roasts and should not be used.

THE PERFECT AGA GOOSE

A 10-12 lb (4.5-5.5kg) goose will feed 8-10 people comfortably and is a popular choice. It is essential to cook a goose on a grill rack in a roasting tin. Do not prick the skin all over but do prick the heavy folds of fat just behind the wings by the back legs. All cooking times are approximate.

WHOLE GOOSE

A whole 10 lb (4.5kg) stuffed goose will take approximately 3 hours total cooking time, a 12 lb (5.4kg) goose $3^1/_2$ hours. Protect the legs and wings with fat bacon and foil, and tent the whole bird with foil leaving a slit in the top by the breastbone during cooking. Roast in an Aga roasting tin on the lowest set of runners in the roasting oven for 1 hour. Then remove the fat that has filled the tin, turn the bird upside down and roast for a further hour. Remove fat and turn back the right side up for 20 minutes, uncovered, to brown. Re-cover with foil and continue roasting until cooked.

BONED & ROLLED GOOSE ROASTS

For roasts such as 'goose banquet rolls', 'three bird roasts' and 'birds within a bird' (a pheasant in a chicken in a goose, etc.) and turkey or duck breasts rolled in a boned goose, fast roast these only using the turkey fast method timings as a guide. Because boned and rolled roasts are so dense, it is essential to ensure that they are thoroughly cooked right to the centre. The use of a meat thermometer is strongly recommended. The slow method is not suitable for these roasts and should not be used.

STRESS-FREE SERVING

TESTING FOR DONENESS

To check that the bird is thoroughly cooked, ideally use a meat thermometer in the thickest portion of the thigh, behind the knee joint next to the body. It should read 70-72°C (158-160°F). Alternatively, pierce with a skewer and check that the juices run clear. If any tinge of pink shows, return to the oven and check again after 20 minutes. A further check is to 'shake hands' with the legs – they should be easy to wiggle in their sockets and the thickest portion of the drumsticks should feel tender when pressed.

KEEPING IT ALL HOT

A cooked turkey or goose will keep hot for a surprisingly long time: a large mass of cooked food contains a lot of stored heat. I like to transfer the cooked bird to a second clean Aga roasting tin so that you have the fat and juices easily available to make the gravy. This is where having extra Aga roasting tins is so useful. Once covered with a double thickness of foil, pile over several clean towels as an insulating jacket, reminiscent of the lagging on a hot water cylinder. On a four oven Aga place on the Warming Plate or hob above the left hand ovens. On a two or three oven Aga use a warm area near your Aga or somewhere away from draughts. Left like this, it will still be piping hot when you sit down for your Christmas meal. More importantly, the bird will have benefited from having a chance to rest while you finish preparing the rest of the meal. Allow a minimum of 30 minutes and a maximum of an hour and a half resting before carving. Fill the Simmering and Warming Ovens several hours before the meal and plan beforehand how best to pack with plates, serving dishes and saucepans. As you finish making the gravy, add the resting juices that will have accumulated below the turkey which by now will be very relaxed. If you have a large turkey, carve half of it in the kitchen, then carry to the dining room with the un-carved side showing so it looks complete.

LEFTOVERS

Once served, cool the cooked bird as quickly as possible and refrigerate the leftover meat, stuffing and gravy. Putting it in an unheated room or animal-proof garage for two hours will allow it to cool sufficiently ready for storing in the refrigerator. It is recommended not to store cold cooked turkey in the refrigerator for more than three days, so freeze what you will not be able to use in that time. Break down the carcass and either make turkey stock or freeze it to make some at a later date. Turkey stock makes fabulous turkey soup and is well worth trying – the result is far superior to any turkey soup you can buy.

COOKING FOR NUMBERS

When a lot of food is needed when cooking for crowds, the Aga really comes into its own. You can produce large quantities of hot food that would be much more difficult, if not impossible, with a conventional cooker. This means you can easily cater for large numbers, but careful planning ahead is necessary. If placing the cooker under a very heavy load, always allow extra time for everything to be cooked. The Simmering Oven can accommodate a large preserving pan and this can be pressed into service for a number of things. A second large pan of cooked food can be kept hot in the Warming Oven with a third placed on the Warming Plate of a 4 oven Aga. Once everything is cooked, and not before, and a further large pan needs to be kept hot and the rest of the cooker is already in use, place the pan on an open Aga toaster on the Simmering Plate. This will allow a thread of heat to keep the pan hot without the contents catching. At a push, a second Aga toaster can be used in this way on the Boiling Plate, but use it in its normal closed position to give a greater air gap between the pan and the intense heat. On many occasions, such as at firework parties, I have used a 2 oven Aga to serve two different hot soups, followed by baked potatoes with a choice of hot fillings for more than 80 people. The pans of soup will keep steadily hot over several hours. I have also cooked one plate pasta suppers for over 120 people on a 4 oven Aga using the know-how described below. From the examples given below you will see the extension of the basic principles that I have already covered. These should give you a good guide on how to approach cooking for larger numbers. Always remember that a substantial mass of food takes a lot longer to heat up and cook. The same is true when re-heating a large quantity of previously prepared food. An equally important point, from a food safety point of view, is to remember that a large mass of food also takes a proportionally longer time to cool down. With high-risk foods such as meat and poultry, it is vital that they are quickly cooled and refrigerated. Ideally, this should happen within two hours from cooking. Do not try and skip this important step in temperature control.

The examples included in the section below have been carefully chosen to show you what is possible with a little thought and preparation. They are representative of scenarios and menus which I have used over many years when the occasion has arisen to press an Aga into service for cooking for larger numbers. These techniques work with the minimum of fuss and should help you in applying the same principles to other favourite recipes. Keep the menu simple and you will soon see how easy it is to entertain for a large crowd.

SOUP

Soup for a crowd can be kept hot without any attention and then brought out when required. Preferably, serve your own soup made from scratch, though quite acceptable results can be obtained by using a good quality catering pack of dried soup and transforming it using good home-made chicken stock and strengthening the main ingredients with some robust additions. For example, add plenty of tomato passata and a little sugar and herbs to tomato soup, or several drained and liquidised tins of asparagus to a vegetable soup. Finish off with a good slug of sherry and a simple garnish. Always save any cream for adding just before serving. Allow $^1/_3$ pint (200ml) per person if serving other food, or $^1/_2$ pt (300ml) if only serving soup and a roll.

BREAD

As well as serving on its own in mugs, soup can also be served with warm crusty bread crisped in the Roasting Oven using bought large baguettes. Home-made onion bread is particularly popular and makes a welcome change. Part-baked baguettes and petits pains can be cooked in 7-10 minutes in the Roasting Oven, but for larger numbers full size ready-baked baguettes are preferable, as over time more than six batches of the part-baked kind will start to take longer to bake as the stored heat is consumed. Baked full size baguettes can simply be heated through just before serving, as can large trays of garlic and herb breads, although allow a little longer for these, swapping the trays around during heating. Allow the equivalent volume of $1^1/_2$ rolls per person. For large numbers I rely on ready-baked baguettes or rolls with part-baked ones in reserve to cook if required.

CASSEROLES AND MEAT SAUCES

Large pans of casseroles and meat sauces such as chilli and Bolognaise sauce can cook and kept hot in the Simmering Oven. If making ahead, it is important after cooking to cool them rapidly. As a large quantity holds its heat, transfer to one or two full size Aga roasting tins and place on cooling racks in a cool place. In this way they can be safely cooled within 2 hours, ready for their contents to be transferred into plastic containers to store in the refrigerator. This is very important in the interests of food safety. An hour before re-heating, take the food out of the refrigerator to allow it to come to room temperature. It is important to ensure that the contents are then brought up to full temperature on the Simmering Plate or on a grid shelf on the floor of the Roasting Oven – check that they are really hot right through before transferring to the Simmering Oven to keep hot, if required. Stirring is therefore important during the re-heating process. Because of this, when making a casserole or sauce for large numbers, I usually do so with no thickening added in the early stages as it is then easier to re-heat rapidly on the Boiling Plate with constant stirring. With no starch from any thickening agent there is therefore no danger of it 'catching' during re-heating. When hot, it can then finally be thickened using beurre manié or your favourite thickening agent. Continue cooking on the Simmering Plate for several minutes. When it has bubbled satisfactorily, transfer to the Simmering Oven to keep hot until required. For casseroles with sliced potato toppings such as Lancashire hot-pot, also see the following section. If necessary, brush the potato with a little salted milk and transfer to the highest set of runners to finish browning the topping.

MEAT, POULTRY AND VEGETABLE PIES

Make the meat filling such as steak and kidney using your normal recipe multiplied up the day before. Transfer to full size Aga roasting tins and cool, as in the above section, within 2 hours and then refrigerate. If necessary, the cold mixture can be transferred into plastic containers. The next day, take the mixture out of the refrigerator an hour before heating to come to room temperature first, in the full size roasting tins. Cover with shortcrust or puff pastry, after first adhering a strip of pastry to the perimeter of the tins using a little cold water. If possible, use several pie funnels to lift the pastry and provide an escape for steam. Apply two coats of eggwash made from beaten egg, a little milk and some salt to provide a good colour. Bake in the Roasting Oven on the lowest set of runners and allow up to 40 minutes. Insert a knife into the centre of the filling and check that it is piping hot. If in doubt, return to the floor of the oven, with a cold plain shelf above if it starts to brown further. A second pie made in another full size Aga roasting tin can then be cooked above the first one, and as the oven will have cooled slightly, the pastry will be fine in this higher position. When the pastry is perfectly cooked, transfer the pie to the floor of the oven if necessary. If a third and fourth pie are to be cooked, follow the same method, but in this case only it is a good idea not to use the Simmering Plate during the baking period for all of the pies. This is because you are introducing a very large amount of cold food that requires a very hot oven to fully cook the pastry and heat the pie filling. This amount of food is in fact comparable to cooking a large 28 lb (13kg) turkey. Cooked pies can be kept hot on the Warming Plate or on a chef's pad or folded cloth on top of the insulated lids if the Simmering Oven is not free. I have found that the Baking Oven is fine for one large pie, but subsequent pies take a lot longer to cook the pastry satisfactorily and it is therefore preferable to use the hotter Roasting Oven.

LAYERED PIES, PASTA AND VEGETABLE BAKES

For shepherd's pie and cottage pie, follow the same principles as in the above method, but start to bake on the floor of the Roasting Oven; also use this method for fish pie. It also works well for lasagne and other assembled pasta recipes and for meat and vegetarian moussaka. If gravy or sauce starts to bubble up around the edges halfway through cooking, move to the lowest set of runners to cut off bottom heat while the potato topping finishes heating and browning. If browned, but not thoroughly re-heated, use a cold plain shelf to protect the pie until the centre is piping hot. Two or three full size Aga roasting tins can be cooked in the Roasting Oven, swapping them around so that they all receive direct heat from the oven floor, browning from the top of the oven and general radiant heat from the middle of the oven. The Baking Oven may also be used, if available, for up to two pies. If necessary, keep a pie hot on an Aga toaster on the floor of the oven and use cold plain shelves to protect higher pies from browning further once they are cooked. In this way once cooked, several pies can be kept hot in the Roasting Oven. After cooking three or four full size Aga roasting tins of food, the oven will have reduced in temperature somewhat so that there will be little danger of food over-browning.

CHICKEN AND STEAKS

Chicken breasts and steaks can be browned and cooked early in the day using the Aga grill pan or on baking trays on the floor and at the top of the oven. They should then be quickly cooled in a single layer on baking trays on cooling racks within 2 hours and then placed in plastic containers in the refrigerator. Twenty-four portions can easily be accommodated in each full size Aga roasting tin, stacked overlapping in rows. If you have room, you can even place them in the roasting tins in the refrigerator. Take the food out of the refrigerator at least an hour before re-heating, to allow it to come to room temperature first. A cold prepared sauce can be poured over the cooked meat or poultry before finishing off in the oven. The whole assembly can be re-heated on the floor of the Roasting Oven to finish cooking and then heated through until piping hot an hour before serving. If necessary, transfer to the Simmering Oven to finish and keep hot until wanted. If cooking a second batch in a full size roasting tin, place this at the same time in the middle of the Roasting Oven and swap the tins half-way through cooking. The floor of the Baking Oven can also be used. Roast chicken pieces are also possible for a medium number of people, but are not recommended when cooking for more than 20 people on a 2 oven Aga or for more that 40-50 on 3 and 4 oven models.

SAUSAGES

Good quality sausages are delicious and are best cooked in large numbers in full size Aga baking trays in a little oil on the floor of the Roasting Oven. A second batch can be grilled in the normal way at the top of the Roasting Oven at the same time and then all kept hot while further batches are finished off. Don't attempt to cook more than a single layer at a time. The Baking Oven may also be used to advantage when cooking sausages for large numbers. Because it is a hot oven but kept at a slightly lower temperature, it is ideal for cooking large trays of thicker sausages. The longer cooking time ensures that the heat has plenty of time to penetrate the sausages ensuring that they are thoroughly cooked. They can then be finished off cosmetically with a quick browning at the top or on the floor of the Roasting Oven. If serving with baps or baguettes, cook a large quantity of slowly softened onions to serve with them. Use butter with a little oil to prevent burning and prepare ahead of time. These are then safe to re-heat by placing the pan in the Simmering Oven 3-4 hours before serving.

RICE

Rice cooked by the Aga absorption method also works well in a large pan. Bring the measured water to the boil on the Boiling Plate with some salt. Add the rice and give one gentle stir to disperse the rice from the base of the pan. Once it has come back to the boil, simmer for 2 minutes before transferring to the Simmering Oven. If your Simmering Oven is full of food, transfer the pan to the Simmering Plate on an open Aga toaster. With this method, it is essential that the lid is not removed until the cooking time has elapsed. Remember that loading the Simmering Plate will have an effect on the Roasting Oven so if necessary cook food requiring the oven at its fullest heat before everything else and cook the rice in this way last. Alternatively, if your Boiling Plate is not being used, follow the traditional method of boiling rice. Bring a large pan of salted water to the boil, using kettles if necessary, and add the rice. Slow boil as directed and then drain in a colander. Pour over several kettles of boiling water to rinse away excess starch. It is best to cook rice and then serve it, or keep it hot for a short time, covered in the Warming or Simmering Ovens.

NOODLES AND PASTA

Noodles that only take four minutes to cook are a boon when you are producing a very large quantity of food for a lot of people. Bring a large pan of water to the boil, and then drop in the noodles and cover with a lid, timing carefully to avoid over-cooking.

Cooking a large quantity of dried pasta requires a little planning but works very well. I have cooked one-plate suppers for over 120 people on a 4 oven Aga many times using the following method. Pans of pasta sauce can first be heated several hours ahead of time and kept hot in the Warming or Simmering Ovens; I would suggest you offer at least two contrasting types. Before cooking the pasta, ensure that all the pans required for cooking are full of hot water (see below). When you are ready to cook the pasta, remove a large pan of sauce from the Simmering Oven and keep hot in the Warming Oven or on top of the Aga. This makes space for a large pan of water for cooking pasta to be transferred to the Simmering Oven to finish cooking. A second large pan of pasta can then be started cooking on the Boiling Plate. Alternatively, that pan could then be transferred to the Simmering Plate to again release the Boiling Plate to accommodate a third large pan.

Heating large quantities of water Water has a high specific heat capacity, that is to say, it takes a lot of energy to bring large 20 pint (11 litre) pans of water from cold to boiling on any domestic cooker. It is therefore vital to get the required number of large pans full of boiling water and to keep them hot in, on or near the Aga until they have all been filled and heated. Then, and only then, add the pasta to each pan in turn on the Boiling Plate. Remember to time each pan carefully to prevent over-cooking; note the exact time when you drop in the dried pasta, as you should calculate the total cooking time from this point rather than from when the pan returns to the boil. Take great care when draining large pans of boiling water.

BAKED POTATOES

Always cook in a single layer. A full size Aga roasting tin of potatoes will take $1^1/_2$-2 hours to cook in the Roasting Oven. If cooking more than a single full size roasting tin of potatoes, allow double the cooking time – the dense mass of potato in the upper tin will act in the same way as a cold plain shelf. Swap the layers around half-way through cooking. Due to the high thermal inertia of potato, baked potatoes for numbers should only be cooked in the Roasting Oven; they will not cook properly in the Baking Oven. For more than two full size roasting tins of potato it is therefore important to cook two oven loads of two tins in succession. Cooked baked potatoes keep hot perfectly for several hours in the Warming and Simmering Ovens.

NEW POTATOES AND MASH

If cooking a large quantity of potatoes in preserving pans, unlike the normal technique of bringing to the boil in cold salted water, it is better to pour over water that has been boiled first. From cold, on any domestic cooker, these would otherwise take a long time to come to the boil and cook.
Once simmering, allow a good 10 minutes before draining and transferring to the Simmering Oven. Allow 50% longer than you would for normal quantities. With new potatoes it is essential to ensure they are all of a similar size, so cut any large ones, if necessary. Once cooked they will keep perfectly hot before finishing as required. For creamy mashed potatoes, mash using a beater in a stand mixer such as a KitchenAid by pre-heating the bowl and beater with boiling water first. On no account use a food processor, as this would turn the mash to an unattractive glue-like consistency. Otherwise enlist help and get them to use a hand masher and plenty of elbow grease. Beat in hot milk, butter and cream with salt and plenty of black and white pepper until light and fluffy. Keep hot in a large buttered container and cover with a lid, or seal with clingfilm to prevent it drying out.

ROOT VEGETABLES

For root vegetables, use the Aga oven steaming method but as with potatoes, start off by pouring over boiling water. Follow the potato method above and allow 50% extra time than usual.
Note that swede can take the longest time to cook so needs to be given a lot longer. This is important if you are cooking a large pan of a mixture of root vegetables to mash. Simply build into your time plan a longer period in the Simmering Oven, or give the pan a longer initial period of boiling first. Once cooked, a large pan of cooked vegetables will keep hot for a long time if wrapped in clean towels, releasing the oven for another purpose. Do this on the Warming Plate on a 4 oven Aga if available. If necessary, once all the food is cooked, use the Simmering Plate and Boiling Plate toaster methods given in the beginning of this section to keep vegetables hot.

GREEN VEGETABLES

To cook large quantities of green vegetables, the best solution is to steam them. Do this when everything else is cooked, just before serving. Place a large collapsible steamer in the base of an Aga preserving pan. Pour in boiling water to almost come up to the base of the steamer. Bring to the boil on the Boiling Plate and add the green vegetables. Keep the water boiling hard to generate a good supply of steam. Place the lid half offset on the pan to contain the steam whilst still allowing excess to escape, along with the sulphurous compounds released from the vegetables. If more than one pan is needed, transfer to the Simmering Plate and start the second on the Boiling Plate. With care, two large pans can be accommodated on each hotplate at the end of the cooking session to steam green vegetables in this way. Because a relatively small amount of water is used, undue heat loss is avoided.

FROZEN VEGETABLES

If you try to cook a substantial amount of frozen vegetables for a large number of people on any domestic cooker you will find that they take a long time to return to the boil after being added to boiling water. The solution is to defrost them partially over several hours on trays before cooking. In this way, you will not be giving the pan such a large cold loading. Using too much water would further compound the loading, so it is important to use only as much water as is necessary to cover them. It is impossible to easily gauge this, so the solution is to place the vegetables in your largest pan first. Do not attempt to fill the pan more than half-full – if necessary repeat with a second batch. Bring a kettle to the boil, and have at least one medium saucepan full of boiling water. Place the vegetable pan on the Boiling Plate, and pour over just enough boiling water to cover by $^{1}/_{2}$ inch (1cm). Add salt and give the vegetables a quick stir. Cover with a lid to help speed the heating process. Once they have come to the boil they will not require much further cooking, so test earlier than normal. Drain and serve.

TINNED VEGETABLES

Tinned sweetcorn is one of the more respectable tinned vegetables, which also re-heats well in a little water. Once heated through it can be drained and kept hot in the Warming or Simmering Ovens or on top of the Aga in one of the ways previously discussed. Tinned tomatoes are also useful in some menus. For example, I find they are welcome when serving lasagne and small baked potatoes, as the liquid keeps things from being too dry on the plate. As they keep hot in the Warming and Simmering Ovens for a long time without deteriorating, they can be heated through early in proceedings. Baked beans are another useful vegetable, and as well as keeping hot perfectly for a very long time, can be partnered with small or large cooked sausages and some suitable sweet or devilled ingredients to make variations on the barbecued baked beans theme, either as a main course for large quantities of people, or as one of several hot fillings for baked potatoes.

BLANCHING VEGETABLES

If you are cooking a large number of vegetables, you may be tempted to try and use the Get Ahead vegetable platter method described earlier in this section. However, the timings required to re-heat sequentially more than one platter, either full size Aga roasting tin or baking tray, mean that there is no benefit in using this technique. The re-heating rapidly technique is designed to work when one platter of food is re-heated to be immediately served piping hot. To re-heat several trays would necessitate keeping the heated trays hot in the Warming or Simmering Ovens as the rest are re-heated on the floor of the Roasting Oven. Foods which have been blanched beforehand do not respond well to this treatment. When cooking vegetables for large numbers, therefore, cooking from scratch is required.

THE AGA AND THE BARBECUE – A PERFECT COMBINATION

The stored reserves of heat found in the Aga are ideal for combining with your barbecue. The biggest advantage is when serving jointed chicken pieces as these take longer to cook than many enthusiastic barbecue chefs imagine. They can be cooked in full size Aga roasting tins in the Roasting Oven until they are at least three-quarters cooked. In the interests of food safety and to ensure thorough cooking, I prefer to cook them fully in the Aga, and then they can be finished off on the barbecue. The use of water-soaked hickory and other wood chips added to the barbecue during this process helps to increase the delicious smoky flavours. Where the barbecue features a hinged canopy, close this to concentrate the smoke. This ensures that even if chicken is only subjected to a final five minutes' barbecue treatment, each batch is beautifully even-coloured as well as being moist and safely cooked within.

After chicken, prioritise those foods to be barbecued which are largest and densest for pre-cooking in the Aga. For sausages, see the notes above. Of course, use the Aga's Warming and Simmering Ovens to keep all the cooked barbecued food hot until everything is perfectly cooked. In this way you and your friends can all sit down together to enjoy a delicious meal on hot plates and all those involved in the preparation can actually enjoy the meal too. To make the menu more interesting, serve juicy cobs of sweetcorn wrapped in foil for your guests to eat as a simple first course. They can cook to perfection in the Roasting Oven. Simply keep in their husks if possible and soak in cold water for 5 minutes before wrapping tightly in foil and placing onto a tray directly on the floor of the Roasting Oven. They will take between 15-20 minutes. If you need the oven for cooking other things and your Boiling Plate is not being used, drop these into fast-boiling salted water and cook until tender. Soften some butter in a dish on the top plate to serve with them.

LIFE'S LITTLE LUXURIES

With an Aga in your kitchen, simple little luxury 'extras' become a matter of daily routine because making them is so easy. Special equipment, like double pans and sterilisers, is not required, and making small batches of delicious preserves is greatly simplified. People with busy and demanding careers miraculously find they have time on occasion to make chutney they would never have attempted with their previous cooker – all because the Aga is always there. Whereas in the past you might have been reluctant to turn your oven on 'specially', with the Aga you are able to tuck a jar of ingredients into your cooker and an hour later be spreading a delicious home-made preserve on to some toast – and you weren't even in the room the whole time it was happening, with not a penny of extra expense. In the final part of this section I share with you a few of my favourites. You will find that they will soon become yours too.

AGA LEMON CURD

Delicious lemon curd can be made in the Simmering Oven without the need for a double boiler or a bowl over simmering water. This wonderful technique for using up surplus egg yolks means that the ingredients can be left to cook with none of the usual stirring or 20 minutes' attention. The other joy is that every piece of equipment used can be placed in the dishwasher: double boilers from making lemon curd are normally horrible to have to clean. You can use most lemon curd recipes, but this is my favourite and calls for a good number of surplus egg yolks. A whole egg is added to give a silky consistency. The recipe is best made in a preserving jar, so use a suitable wide-mouthed 'Le Parfait' or 'Kilner' jar. Alternatively, a Pyrex jug or basin may be used. Place 2 oz (50g) butter and 6 oz (150g) caster sugar in the jar. If it has a rubber sealing gasket, remove this from the lid. Close and place the jar to heat gently in the Simmering Oven for 30 minutes. Meanwhile, remove the lemon zest from a large, unwaxed lemon and reserve – I use a highly efficient Microplane. Then place the lemon in the Roasting Oven for three minutes before squeezing to extract the most juice. Add the zest and juice to the jar and leave for a further 30 minutes. Give the mixture a quick stir to ensure that the sugar has dissolved into the lemon juice. Working quickly, add 3 yolks and 1 whole egg and whisk for a minute with a rotary whisk. Replace the lid and return to the Simmering Oven for 1-1¼ hours. Give the curd a final stir and leave to cool. Replace the sealing gasket and store in the refrigerator. This will then keep for up to three weeks.

AGA CHOCOLATE FUDGE

To make Aga chocolate fudge, place 12 oz (350g) of chopped plain chocolate with 12 oz (350g) smooth peanut butter into a Pyrex bowl in the Simmering Oven for 30 minutes. Stir to make sure that the chocolate is completely melted. Working quickly, add a 14 oz (400g) tin of sweetened condensed milk and 1 teaspoon of vanilla extract Pour into a lined 8-inch (20cm) square tin. Chill and cut into 1-inch pieces. Variations with glacé cherries, crystallised ginger and rum-soaked raisins are possible. If preferred, just before the mixture is fully set, the cubes can be gently rolled into balls and then dusted with drinking chocolate or caster sugar.

AGA CANDIED PEEL

Making candied peel can be greatly simplified by using the following Aga method. Traditional recipes take many more days and increase the sugar concentration in the syrup every other day. The Aga method is much simpler and more practical. Orange, lemon and grapefruit skins are all suitable. Wash the peel and just cover with cold water. Add a pinch of salt and bring to the boil on the Boiling Plate and after 3 minutes cover and transfer to the Simmering Oven for 2 hours. It is best to prepare the peels in separate batches so that the flavours remain distinct. With grapefruit only, it is necessary to change the water 2 or 3 times to remove the bitterness. For the next process, first make some stock syrup, which is also useful for making sorbets and fondant for desserts and icings.

To make stock syrup, cover 2 lbs (900g) of granulated sugar in a large heavy pan with 1¼ pints (700ml) cold water. Allow to dissolve without stirring on the Simmering Plate. When every grain of sugar has completely dissolved, transfer to the Boiling Plate and once boiling, return to the Simmering Plate and simmer for 3-4 minutes. Cool and store in the refrigerator.

Drain the peel and place in a pan just large enough to contain it with a small amount of headroom. Just cover with stock syrup and bring to the boil on the Boiling Plate, then cover and transfer to the Simmering Oven for 30 minutes. Remove and leave to soak in the syrup in a cool place. Repeat the process the next day. On the third day, after the slow simmer in the oven, transfer to the Simmering Plate and slow boil to allow as much of the syrup as possible to be finally absorbed while syrup gradually concentrates. This will take about 10-15 minutes and needs careful watching. Place the peel on a wire rack to drain over a baking tray. Any syrup left over can be used for further batches. When the peel has dried out, store into glass jars in a cool, dark place.

AGA CHOCOLATE ORANGE SLICES

Candied peel also makes a delicious sweet, especially when strips are dipped into dark chocolate to make chocolate orange petits fours.

For a special effect, follow the above method using unwaxed oranges, sliced 1/4 inch (5mm) thick.

AGA MARRONS GLACES

Making preserved chestnuts is usually a complicated and time-consuming art which is not normally worth attempting at home. With the Aga Simmering Oven there is a simple way to make your own, that once started, only takes a few minutes a day for a week or so to produce very credible results. To make the marrons, poach cooked, peeled chestnuts in stock syrup (see Aga Candied Peel above). They are very delicate and should be handled extremely carefully. Just cover the nuts and bring to a gentle simmer on the Simmering Plate. After 5 minutes, transfer to the Simmering Oven for 30 minutes. Return to the Simmering Plate and give them a final 10 minutes' slow boiling. Allow to cool in the syrup. When quite cold, carefully transfer to a glass preserving jar using a slotted spoon. Strain the syrup to remove small pieces of nut and fill the jar to within 1/2 inch (1cm) of the top. Close with the normal sealing gasket. The next day, whilst making your evening meal, place the jar in the Simmering Oven for 2-3 hours. Remove and allow to cool and store in a cool place. Repeat this for up to 10 days, as necessary – with each processing, the nuts will gently darken and begin to look semi-transparent. Store in a cool, dry place. When wanted, lift each one carefully out and allow surplus syrup to drain on a wire rack. Place each whole dry nut in petits fours cases for serving. The syrup can be strained again and used to give a delicate chestnut flavour to desserts.

TEN CLASSIC AGA RECIPES

The first two recipes here are those that are most often requested. The shortbread is my own variation on the classic recipe. I prefer to use cornflour but ground rice or semolina may be used instead, which gives a slightly crunchier texture. The one main variation that I occasionally turn to is the addition of quartered glacé cherries. The second recipe was devised by Dawn Roads, my colleague at Aga, and it makes the best ever flapjacks. She and I endlessly ring the changes with different flavours and ingredients. These are both extra quick to make as you can use 250g packs of butter as weights when using balance scales – the best scales you can use.

AGA SHORTBREAD

1 lb (500g) butter
8 oz (250g) caster sugar
1 lb (500g) plain flour
8 oz (250g) cornflour
8 oz (250g) glacé cherries (variation)

Have the butter at room temperature, in a bowl near the Aga for an hour or so. Cream the butter with the sugar until light and fluffy. Gradually work in the flours. The all-in-one method may also be used in a KitchenAid with the beater or a food processor. If using cherries, rinse these of their syrup in hot water, drain and carefully pat dry. Cut into quarters and work into the finished dough. Pile into a large Aga baking tray lined with Bake-O-Glide or baking parchment. Once the mixture has been roughly levelled, cover with a sheet of clingfilm and press down into place using a clean preserve jar or can as a small roller, then prick well. The mixture can also be pressed into several 7 inch (18cm) lined circular tins to quickly make petticoat tails. Make a circle with a small biscuit cutter in the centre before marking out the outer section before pricking. Alternatively, this mixture can be rolled out on a well floured board and cut into shapes with cutters.

On a 2 oven Aga, cook on the grid shelf on the floor of the Roasting Oven with a cold plain shelf on the second set of runners above. Bake for 15-20 minutes, turning once, until a very light golden brown. Transfer to the middle of the Simmering Oven for a further 20-40 minutes.

On a 3 and 4 oven Aga, cook on the lowest set of runners in the Baking Oven. Bake for 25-30 minutes until a very light golden brown. Transfer to the Simmering Oven for a further 15-25 minutes.

Tastes vary, and the final cooking time will depend on whether you prefer a 'just cooked, but not crisp' texture, or more of a biscuit type finish.

AGA FLAPJACKS

Use a table knife to cut into fingers, squares or triangles while still warm. Allow to cool and then separate into pieces and store in an airtight tin.

9 oz (250g) butter
9 oz (250g) light brown sugar
9 oz (250g) golden syrup
1 lb 1 oz (500g) rolled oats
3 oz (75g) walnut pieces
4 oz (100g) chopped dates
a few drops orange oil or juice

Or, for my Apricot and Ginger Variation:
Substitute the walnuts, dates and orange oil or juice with 4 oz (100g) chopped apricots, 3 oz (75g) chopped glacé or crystallised ginger and 1 tsp ground ginger.

Melt the butter with the syrup in a large pan on the Simmering Plate. Stir in the sugar and when dissolved, add the oats and other ingredients. Pile into a large Aga baking tray lined with Bake-O-Glide. Press down lightly with the back of a wooden spoon.

On a 2 oven Aga, cook on a grid shelf on the floor of the Roasting Oven with a cold plain shelf on the second set of runners above. Bake for 20-25 minutes, turning once, until a light golden brown. **On a 3 and 4 oven Aga**, cook on the lowest set of runners in the Baking Oven. Bake for 20-25 minutes until a light golden brown.

Allow to cool for 5 minutes and then use a table knife to mark into fingers or squares.

AGA OVEN-BUSTER YORKSHIRE PUDDINGS

The increased protein in the form of extra eggs is one of the secrets that guarantees a perfect rise, together with chilling the batter before it is used – the thermal shock from cold into smoking hot fat causes them to spring into action. This quantity may be cooked in a number of different tins. The half size Aga roasting tin is excellent for a traditional pudding or use two Aga Yorkshire pudding trays. Another option is to use a bun tray or several mini muffin trays for easy Mini Sunday Lunch canapés (*see* page 102).

4 oz (100g) plain flour, sifted
2 whole large eggs beaten with an extra yolk
$^{1}/_{2}$ pt (300ml) cold semi-skimmed milk
$^{1}/_{2}$ tsp salt
a large pinch of white pepper
a grinding of fresh black pepper
a little oil or good beef dripping

Sieve the flour twice to aerate it well and either make by hand using a bowl, where you make a well and gradually whisk in the eggs and milk followed by the seasonings; or alternatively place the eggs and half the milk in a processor and add the flour and process, scrape down and when smooth, add the remainder of the milk with the machine still running. Chill in a jug before use.

Heat a little of your chosen fat or oil (this is one of the few occasions I like to use beef dripping to give an authentic beef back note) in the metal tins on the floor of the Roasting Oven. Place a grid shelf on the second or third set of runners down, so that the tins can be placed as high as you dare in the oven, but leaving just enough space for the raised puddings not to adhere to the roof of the oven if not using an Aga roasting tin. Take the batter out of the refrigerator and whisk in a tablespoon of cold water; it should be the consistency of single cream. When the fat is good and hot, quickly pour or ladle in the batter and immediately return to the oven; either on the shelf if using tins or onto the second set of runners if using the Aga roasting tin. Push well to the back of the oven to get a strong blast of heat. Allow 15 minutes approximately for small individual ones, and up to 35 minutes for one large pudding. Check after three-quarters of the anticipated cooking time – opening the door will not cause them to collapse. The puddings cook best in a really hot oven and, like many Aga writers, I have always maintained that baking them first thing in the morning, before cooking anything else, gives the very best results. They can then be allowed to cool and placed in a cool place, covered with a clean tea towel. Just before serving your meal, return them to the Roasting Oven to reheat for three or four minutes before rushing to table.

AGA OVERNIGHT CHEESECAKE

This recipe was popularised when it was featured on an American Aga sales video in the 1980's. The recipe appears regularly on the Internet with minor variations, but it's the Aga Simmering Oven technique that makes it so special. If you have difficulty finding soured cream you can easily make your own by stirring a little lemon juice into double cream and leaving it at room temperature for an hour. In either case, for the best results use half soured cream and half full-fat fromage frais. This is because American soured cream is different from that sold in the UK, which is not as thick.

I sometimes take a cheesecake to demonstrations to show the perfect top which never cracks – something notoriously difficult to achieve in conventional ovens.

14 oz (400g) digestive biscuits
5 oz (150g) melted butter
2 lb (1kg) curd or cream cheese
6 oz (175g) caster sugar
2 large eggs, beaten
1 tsp vanilla extract
2 tbsp cornflour
8 fl oz (190ml) soured cream
Whipped cream and fruit to garnish

Crush the biscuits in a plastic bag, or use a food processor, and mix in the melted butter. Press well into the base and sides of a well-greased and lined $9^1/_2$ inch (24cm) Aga spring-form tin. Chill in the freezer. Beat together the cheese and sugar until pale and thick. Beat in the eggs, and then the vanilla extract and cornflour, gently fold in the sour cream and pour into the prepared tin. Cook on a cold plain shelf on the grid shelf on the floor of the Roasting Oven for 7-8 minutes until the filling is starting to set. Remove from the oven and cover with baking foil. Transfer to a grid shelf on the floor of the Simmering Oven. The cheesecake will be ready in approximately six hours. Once you have determined the exact cooking time in your Aga, you can cook this cheesecake overnight, putting it in the coolest oven before retiring to bed. Remove it first thing next morning (on a 4 oven cooker the Warming Oven should be used).

AGA RICE PUDDING

Sir Robert Watson-Watt, early inventor and pioneer of RADAR, describes in his autobiography, 'Three Steps to Victory' his time developing the secret technology during the 1930s at Bawdsey Manor in Suffolk. Describing the kitchen there he adds in passing, 'it did now house the Aga cooker whose economic virtues have been widely and justly prized, but whose unique distinction in making the best rice pudding in the world is insufficiently documented.' Here is the recipe from 'A Recipe Book for the Aga Cooker' from the 1930's. Some aficionados insist on stirring in at least one skin before giving a final application of freshly grated nutmeg. I certainly often use creamy Channel Islands milk or add a small tin of evaporated milk to this recipe to enrich the mixture and improve the creaminess wonderfully.

$1^1/_2$-2 oz (40-55g) pudding rice
1 oz (25g) sugar
1 pt (600ml) full cream milk
$^1/_2$ oz (15g) butter
freshly grated nutmeg

Put the well-washed rice, sugar, milk and butter into a pie dish and allow to stand for as long as possible, and for at least several hours. Sprinkle on the nutmeg. Stand the dish in a half size roasting tin and hang on the second set of runners in the Roasting Oven for 20-30 minutes, or until a brown skin has formed and the milk boils; remove from the tin and transfer to the Simmering Oven for $1^1/_2$-2 hours.

AGA DROP SCONES

This and the next recipe come from a 1940's Aga recipe book, the same text of which was in print for more than forty years. A lot of the recipes may seem rather plain for modern tastes, but there are still some gems worth reviving. Both these are thriftily designed to be able to make use of sour milk as a change. The drop scones, with slightly more ingredients than modern recipes, are well worth trying occasionally, as they include separate acid and alkali ingredients. This produces a totally different, puffier result that makes for an interesting change. The girdle scones are also quick to make and popular with children learning to cook.
I am frequently asked for these classic recipes by people savouring fond memories of eating these delicious Aga teatime treats from many years ago.

8 oz (225g) plain flour
$^{1}/_{2}$ tsp salt
$^{1}/_{2}$ tsp bicarbonate of soda
$^{1}/_{2}$ tsp cream of tartar
1 egg, beaten
2 tsp golden syrup
$^{1}/_{2}$ pt (300ml) scant sour milk (if fresh milk is used, increase the cream of tartar to 1 tsp)

If your Simmering Plate is a little on the hot side, raise the lid for a few minutes while you make the batter. Sift the dry ingredients into a bowl. Beat the egg and add to the measured milk and syrup. Now mix all to a smooth batter and leave to stand. Lightly oil the Simmering Plate and drop on tablespoonfuls of the batter and cook on both sides, turning when bubbles appear. Keep hot in a folded napkin and serve warm with syrup.

AGA SCOTCH GIRDLE SCONES

8 oz (225g) plain flour
$^{1}/_{2}$ tsp bicarbonate of soda
$^{1}/_{2}$ tsp cream of tartar
$^{1}/_{2}$ tsp salt
1 tsp golden syrup
$^{1}/_{4}$ pt (150ml) sour milk

Sift together the dry ingredients, add the syrup to the milk and mix to a soft consistency. Turn onto a floured board, knead quickly and lightly until smooth. Roll to $^{1}/_{2}$ inch (1cm) thick and mark into 8. Grease the Simmering Plate with a little oil on a piece of kitchen paper. Cook the scones for 4-6 minutes on each side.

AGA QUEEN OF PUDDINGS

Here is the 1950's Aga recipe for a delicious and easy traditional British pudding. It is still one of my all-time favourites.

2 oz (50g) white breadcrumbs
1/2 pint (300ml) milk
1 oz (25g) butter
grated rind of a lemon
2 eggs
4 oz (115g) caster sugar
2 tbsp jam

Bring the milk and butter to the boil on the Simmering Plate and pour over the breadcrumbs. Add an ounce (25g) of the sugar and the lemon rind and cool slightly. Add the egg yolks and stir and allow to soak for 30 minutes. Pour into a buttered pie dish and stand in a half size roasting tin and hang on the runners in the centre of the Roasting Oven until set – allow about 20-30 minutes. Take out, cool slightly, and spread with jam. To make the meringue, whisk the egg whites stiffly, fold in the remaining sugar a teaspoonful at a time, and pile on to the top of the pudding. Return to the Roasting Oven for two or three minutes to colour slightly and then transfer to the Simmering Oven for about an hour to set the meringue.

MERINGUES

These are very easy in the Aga, if you follow the following technique. The principal reasons for failure include: not measuring the sugar accurately, adding the sugar too soon, or whisking it in too fast. This amount makes enough to fill a lined plain shelf with pyramids, shells or nests.

3 large egg whites
6 oz (175g) caster sugar
a pinch of salt

Take a glass, china or metal bowl (copper if you are a classically trained chef!) that is scrupulously clean and grease free. Avoid plastic at all costs as it impossible to get these completely grease free. Separate each egg and allow absolutely none of any yolk to contaminate the whites. Add a small pinch of salt and whisk with a grease-free whisk. Preferably use an electric whisk – I use my KitchenAid mixer. Once in soft peaks add the sugar with the mixer running, a teaspoonful at a time until it is all incorporated. Pipe or spoon onto Bake-O-Glide or baking parchment.

Slide onto the lowest set of runners in the Simmering Oven for 1-2 1/2 hours. Lift the meringues off and place upside down and transfer the baking sheet to a Chef's Pad or folded tea towel on top of the closed Simmering Plate lid. The Warming Oven on 4 oven cookers may also be used for a longer period.

AGA PAVLOVA

This is a recipe I get asked for several times a week. If you use the following method you will make pavlovas the envy of experts. The ratio of caster sugar to egg white is simply 2 oz (55g) per large egg white. As when making meringues, it is vitally important to use a clean, grease-free bowl. I recommend using a glass or metal bowl with a metal whisk. A KitchenAid mixer and whisk is perfect for the task. Add the carefully separated egg white to the bowl with a small pinch of salt, which helps break up the albumen. Start whisking at a slow speed for half a minute and then increase to full speed. I find there is time to quickly weigh out the sugar while the whites are whisking. For an 8 inch (20cm) pavlova, three egg whites, or four if making a larger 10 inch (25cm) pavlova for a buffet table. As soon as the egg whites are stiff, add the sugar a teaspoon at a time, with the mixer still whisking. In a cup, mix together 1 level teaspoon of cornflour, 1 teaspoon of malt vinegar and 1 teaspoon of vanilla extract. Stir to make a smooth cream and whisk this in. Pile the mixture on to Bake-O-Glide or lightly oiled baking parchment on a cold plain shelf in a circle. Work the mixture as you spread it out to create a crown with a depressed centre and an outer edge forming a thick raised rim. Place in the Simmering Oven for 1-1½ hours until it is firm to the touch; it should ideally have a marshmallow-like centre, still quite soft and gooey. The exact timing varies slightly from one Aga to another and also to suit your personal taste. Sometimes you will find you will need to invert the pavlova carefully and return it to the oven for longer – when it has dried out further the parchment will then peel off more easily indicating that it is ready for use. Place on a serving plate and pile a generous ½ pint (300ml) of whipped double or whipping cream. Top with your choice of fresh fruit and dredge with sieved icing sugar. I particularly like the classic kiwi fruit or fresh peach version as well as raspberry and strawberry variations. Use raspberry or mint leaves to garnish clusters of fruit around the edge of the crown.

If you wish to make a pavlova some days ahead of time, either freeze it to keep it in perfect condition, or dry it out more fully in the Simmering Oven and then store in an air-tight tin in a cool larder or cupboard. When it is used, assemble with the fruit and cream, several hours in advance. This will give the filling a chance to re-hydrate the centre to create a soft and marshmallow-like centre.

6. CLEANING, MAINTENANCE AND LAUNDRY

Look after your Aga, and it will look after you. Most people know someone with an Aga that is still giving faithful service after many decades of service. This section looks at how you can ensure your Aga achieves just that, from cleaning safely the whole of the cooker to what to look for when having it serviced, enabling you to look after your Aga and maximise the benefits of the year-on-year economy that an Aga can provide. If you are thinking of installing an Aga for the first time, pitfalls to avoid and advice on building the cooker into the design of your kitchen are included. You can also learn the secret of how to use the gentle warmth from the Aga to help with family laundry – drying, airing and even undertaking a certain amount of basic ironing.

CLEANING YOUR AGA

HELLO AGA. GOODBYE OVEN CLEANING.

In a recent survey, 36% of homeowners in Britain said that cooker cleaning was their most hated domestic chore. The good news is that your Aga is house-trained from the moment it's installed. That's because the hotplates and cast-iron ovens help to keep themselves clean. The cast-iron surfaces remain permanently hot and spills simply get burnt to a very fine carbon dust, which is easily cleared away with a stiff brush. Unlike a conventional cooker with countless removable burners, spillage wells, pan supports and loose chrome parts that have to be taken apart and washed, there are no fiddly bits and pieces to worry about. In fact the only things that can be removed are the oven doors which simply lift off – how easy is that? All that is usually needed to keep the vitreous enamelled surfaces bright and clean is a daily rub over with a damp soapy cloth followed immediately with clean dry cloth to prevent streaks. Aga E-Cloths are also very useful for dusting or, when damp, for wiping over the enamel.

Although the Aga is a very easy cooker to keep clean, my best advice on cleaning an Aga is to 'clean as you go'. Always keep a damp cloth handy when cooking to wipe up spills as they happen. Acidic foods such as milk and fruit juice can damage vitreous enamel, so this is especially important when making preserves. This simple piece of advice is the key to keeping your Aga pristine. If you understand how to use the cooker correctly, it should not become that dirty in the first place. Use the ovens when cooking foods that splash and the top of the cooker will be kept clean: for example, once food has been added to a grill pan, transfer this to the floor of the Roasting Oven to continue cooking. Similarly, use the floor of the oven for shallow frying foods. When cooking foods that tend to splatter, push the roasting tin or cast iron dish towards the very back of the oven. This makes full use of the oven capacity and helps keep the door lining clean. If cooking something on a hot plate which will splash or spit a lot, prop a cold plain shelf up against the open lid to protect from mess. Alternatively, use an Aga Bake-O-Glide Splash Guard. This is designed for hanging over the front of an open insulated lid to protect it from splashes whilst using a wok or sauté pan for frying. Finally, always keep a wire brush nearby to remind you to keep the hotplates scrupulously clean. The Aga classic hotplate brush has a handle on top that makes it particularly easy to use for this purpose. Aga Specialists stock a wide range of suitable cleaning materials and cloths, and there is also an Aga Cleaning Kit available.

CAST IRON OVENS (ALL MODELS)

Any food spilled or splashed in these ovens is automatically carbonised by the heat of the oven and quickly disappears – the hot Roasting and Baking Ovens are genuinely self-cleaning. They merely need to be brushed out occasionally with a long-handled stiff brush. If necessary, use the wire brush that is supplied with every new Aga to brush the oven floor clear of any deposits. I have to confess that this is something I only do once a year when my cooker is turned off for its annual service. Once it is cold, I remove any shelves from the ovens and use a vacuum cleaner on the cold cooker. If you have an Aga with ovens that have become slightly rusty after not being used for a long period, you will find it is easiest to brush them clean when the cooker is warming up after it is lit. You may wish to clean the metal oven tunnels which are found between the hot oven castings and the front plate, although a lot of owners simply leave cleaning these. Modern models have stainless steel tunnels whilst older cookers have aluminium tunnels. Clean these using Aga Chrome and Steel Cleaner or a mild cream cleanser on aluminium, then buff with a dry cloth.

Use thick gauntlets to lift off the doors for cleaning. Make sure you don't get the doors mixed up, as each one is hand-finished with the hinge pins carefully adjusted to ensure each one makes a perfect fit with the front plate. Once they have cooled upside-down on a towel, the aluminium linings may be cleaned. Use a mild cream cleanser or a damp soap-filled wire pad. Use a gentle action working in one direction. Wipe clean with a wet cloth and dry well. Never use any proprietary oven cleaners as these invariably contain caustic components which could cause damage to the aluminium. Also, on no account should you submerge the oven door in water as this would damage the internal insulation. Carefully replace the doors on their hinges.

LEFT-HAND OVENS (4 OVEN AGA ONLY)

The two left-hand ovens on a 4 oven Aga are made of sheet steel. Although they rarely get dirty, wipe them out with a soapy cloth and buff dry.

Any food spills can be cleaned using a mild cream cleanser or a soap-filled pad.

ENAMEL SURFACES

Splashes and spills on the vitreous enamel should be wiped away with a damp cloth as soon as possible. Use Aga Enamel Cleaner regularly, applying it with a damp cloth. It is not always understood that it is important to leave it for a good five to ten minutes to allow it to hydrolyse the grease and deposits – it's a mistake to merely 'wipe on and wipe off'. If left to do its job, all the dirt and grease will then easily come off with a quick wipe with another damp cloth. A final buff with an absorbent towel is then all that is required to bring it back to its legendary deep shine. A little traditional wax furniture polish or silicone car polish may be sparingly applied occasionally. Apply, leave to dry and then give a final buff. Sometimes spills become burned on to the enamel and these deposits over time can build up. This can happen particularly after years of over-using the hotplates without keeping on top of things. What I call the 'bow tie' area between the two hotplates can become thickly encrusted. With care, use a not too coarse soap-filled wire pad, using a very light action, to avoid scratching the enamel. Never use any proprietary oven cleaners as these invariably contain caustic components which could damage the enamel. If you have canine or feline Aga worshippers, owners of oil and gas models will need to periodically check behind the burner door and around the enamel flue chamber for accumulated hair and fluff. Gently remove with a soft brush between servicing but don't be tempted to use a vacuum cleaner behind the burner door in case this could affect the burner.

Note Some components such as the rail brackets and side panels are powder coated and nothing abrasive should be used on them, not even Aga Enamel Cleaner. A warm soapy cloth and a soft cloth are best here.

INSULATED LIDS

The knack to cleaning hot plate lids is to leave them up for a while to cool down a little.
Then place a cold plain shelf on top of a small grill rack positioned on the hotplate. This will protect you from the heat while you are cleaning inside the cooled lids. Aga Cleaning Paste or a damp soap-filled wire pad can be used to clean the inside of the Simmering Plate lid. Use a gentle circular action then wipe clean with a damp cloth and dry well. The Boiling Plate lid is, to a large extent, self-cleaning due to the high temperature of the hotplate below. If you place the spout of a kettle facing the hotplate lid the steam will also help keep it clean. Just an occasional wipe will keep it in a pristine condition. Clean enamel parts of the lids with Aga Enamel Cleaner and chrome or stainless steel parts with Aga Chrome and Steel Cleaner. Apply with a damp soapy cloth, buffing finally with a soft dry towel. Do not use any scouring pads or soap-filled wire pads here as they would cause damage. Electric overnight heat storage Aga cookers feature a special self-cleaning lining inside the Boiling Plate lid which should not be treated with cleaning products. Some early

oil-fired and solid fuel Aga cookers also have this lining (it is obvious if it is fitted as the surface is different from the normal plain aluminium found on the Simmering Plate lid).

HOTPLATES

Keep hotplates clean by brushing with the wire brush supplied with your Aga. Absolutely clean hotplates are essential to ensure efficient heat transfer to saucepans and kettles. Don't be afraid to use a wire brush with some force on the hotplates to remove any stubborn stains – you can't damage the surface. Use either type of Aga wire brush; I particularly like the Aga classic hotplate brush as the handle is easy to hold and keeps your knuckles safely out of the way while brushing. If liquids boil over or spill around the hotplates, disappearing under the top plate, don't worry, they will soon evaporate without damage. Obviously try to remove the excess as soon as it has spilt, using a cloth. What remains will burn off and can be removed later with a wire brush. On the Boiling Plate this can be done after a few minutes, but on the Simmering Plate leave the lid down for at least 30 minutes and the deposits will dry out ready for brushing. Once you have made toast on the Boiling Plate, brush away the toast crumbs left behind as soon as possible so that the hotplate is always clean and ready for use.
The insulating rings around each hotplate can be carefully removed for cleaning, but don't get them mixed up and it is essential that they are replaced back in exactly the same position. There is often a small mark which should face towards the rear of the cooker so that they sit without rocking.
It is wise to leave this for when the cooker is being serviced. Ask the engineer to remove them when he is working on the cooker so you can clean them for him to replace before he leaves.

WARMING PLATE

On older 4 oven cookers the Warming Plate is made from plain aluminium and can be cleaned using a mild cream cleanser – if necessary you can remove the four screws and lift it off should you want to give it a spring-clean. More recent cookers have a hard anodised aluminium version and this is permanently fixed. Clean using a damp soapy cloth.

KETTLES

To boil efficiently, keep your Aga kettle free from limescale deposits. To ensure continued peak performance, get into the habit of regularly descaling your kettle with an approved product such as Kettle Klear. Get into the regular discipline of doing this; the frequency of this will depend on the hardness of your water.

SAUCEPANS

To easily and simply clean stubborn deposits from burnt stainless steel saucepans, cover with Coca-Cola and bring to the boil on the Simmering Plate. Cover and transfer to the Simmering Oven for 10 minutes and then lightly agitate with a nylon brush and rinse clean. Alternatively, fill with warm water and add a little biological detergent powder. Leave for some hours or overnight to loosen the debris, wash and rinse thoroughly. The second technique is safe in aluminium saucepans.

PROTECT YOUR AGA

When you take delivery of a new Aga, do make every member of the family 'Aga Aware'. Explain that it is important to be especially careful with two parts of the Aga. Never drag pans across the enamel as this will quickly scratch the surface, and never place things directly on the closed lids. Either use Aga chef's pads or a folded tea towel to protect the lids. Many owners decide to make it a family rule from day one to agree not to place kettles or anything really heavy, such as roasting tins full of food on top of the lids. Keep a trivet free on the work top next to the Aga. If you need to place something on the top plate, a few small cork mats are useful, or use a piece of kitchen paper to protect the enamel. When guests come to stay, gently point this out on their arrival and your Aga will keep its pristine looks for many years to come.

SWITCHING OFF YOUR AGA

When should you turn off your cooker? If I am going to be away for just a couple of days I leave my Aga just as it is, gently keeping the chill off the whole of the house. If your Aga has a boiler fitted, it can be a good idea to turn the cooker down slightly or to the pilot, but if you have the recommended size of hot water cylinder it should be perfectly safe to leave the system at the normal setting even when no hot water is being used.
I never turn my Aga down and I am away a great deal on business. It is so welcoming when I return home, in the depths of winter, or on a dull summer's day for that matter, to a warm kitchen and plenty of hot water. During periods of extended absence, Aga recommend turning the cooker off. Alternatively, you can turn the cooker down so that it is still on, but at a much lower setting. For an oil fired model, the simple way to do this is to switch off the electrical supply and the cooker will drop down to its low fire setting. For other models it is necessary to retard the thermostat instead. If I am going away for a fortnight in the summer then I will merely turn it down. A cooker that is left running on a low setting comes back to full heat in a much shorter time than one lit from cold, so if you turn it back to its normal setting as soon as you return, within an hour you can still prepare a simple meal or snack. If the cooker is to be left cold for a long period of time, especially if in a damp environment, protect the hotplates from any danger of rusting by lightly smearing them with a little oil or petroleum jelly. Cover with cling film to prevent this drying before closing the lids. Be sure to remove and wipe clean before turning on the cooker. The procedure for switching off your Aga varies according to model – see the Operating Instructions for your particular model.

SERVICING AND MAINTENANCE

An Aga should give you many years of trouble-free service. I have cooked on several cookers that are still going strong after seventy years' uninterrupted use, still running on coke. Part of the reason for this is that they have been looked after well.
All models require routine servicing and maintenance to ensure they continue to run safely and efficiently, so make sure you have your cooker maintained regularly. This is an annual service for gas, and every six months for oil. For electric models, the night storage Aga should have an annual electrical safety check and inspection; a five-year safety check is all that is required for the low maintenance 13 Amp models. Solid fuel models require their internal flueways to be cleaned by the owner monthly, with a six-monthly sweeping of the connecting flue pipe. The chimney should be swept annually. Although the monthly cleaning is easily performed by the owner, it is recommended that an approved engineer carries out a periodic full service.

Turn off your Aga the night before a service – see the Operating Instructions. Then open the lids and doors before going to bed to allow the cooker to cool down for the engineer to work on it the following day (a hot cooker cannot be safely serviced). A full Aga service includes a comprehensive list of twelve checks that are made to ensure that your cooker continues to operate safely at peak efficiency. These are listed below:

- *The operation of all functional controls and components are checked*
- *The safety devices are thoroughly tested*
- *The correct oil flow rates and gas pressures are confirmed*
- *The burner parts and internal flueways are cleaned*
- *The rope seals and gaskets are inspected/ replaced*
- *The operation of insulated lids and doors are adjusted*
- *The level of insulation is verified and, if necessary, topped up*
- *The oil line and storage tanks are given a visual safety check*
- *The gas soundness is thoroughly checked*
- *The integrity and safety of electrical connections and insulation are checked*
- *The flue system and correct ventilation are checked*
- *Circulation and/or oven venting fans are cleaned*

Refer to the Operating Instructions supplied with your Aga, or contact your Aga Specialist who has a team of specially trained service engineers who can service and maintain your cooker. They will also carry the full range of genuine Aga spare parts. In my opinion it is a false economy not to have your Aga serviced by an Aga-trained and approved engineer.

BUYER BEWARE!

When you are deciding to purchase an Aga, it can be tempting to consider a second-hand or reconditioned cooker, thinking that it would be a bargain. There are certainly some worthwhile second-hand cookers to be found, but understandably they are not very plentiful. If you were to go this route, you should only consider a cooker that is still running on its original fuel and that you have seen working. Preferably, get it inspected by a trained engineer. It would need to be professionally dismantled and then reassembled by trained engineer. An Aga should never be moved in one piece as this would almost certainly cause expensive damage to the internal components. The cooker must be stripped down before being carefully packed and moved. Reconditioned cookers are neither always the bargain that you might imagine, when you work out the full extra costs involved concerning delivery, installation, buying all the accessories separately – see the checklist below. There is unlikely to be the back-up and aftercare that you are assured when you buy a new Aga with its 5-year guarantee. If in doubt seek professional advice from an Aga-trained engineer before parting with any money, as you can make an expensive mistake if you are not careful. Invariably when you examine the true cost of second-hand and reconditioned models there is often very little saving over buying from new.

CONVERTED AGA COOKERS

If an Aga is converted from one fuel to another, typically solid fuel to oil or sometimes gas, heat distribution within the cooker may be different, and oven temperatures will often be at considerable variance to those found in a new Aga. This, of course, is not apparent until it is fired up and you try and cook on it. Often a converted cooker isn't fitted with a thermostat, merely a manual control is provided in its place. This means that it has to be constantly manually adjusted, and you lose the automatic control that is central to getting the best and most economical service out of an Aga. An even worse problem is that the Simmering Oven is invariably too cool for slow cooking and therefore just becomes a hot cupboard capable of only warming plates. Without automatic thermostatic control or a correctly functioning Simmering Oven, a converted Aga is incomplete – a shadow of the real thing, sadly emasculated of its finest features. It is for this reason that Aga understandably do not recommend reconditioning or converting Aga cookers. Every Aga contains over 500 different parts and specialist knowledge is required to ensure that it will work correctly with the correct heat distribution to the different parts of the cooker. With more than 20 different models to choose from, each type of modern Aga is individually designed and dedicated to obtain the maximum performance from its particular fuel source. Many of the major internal components vary considerably between models, fuels and flue types. To change from one fuel to another is not just a case of substituting a burner but involves a considerable degree of rebuilding which is rarely cost-effective.

Attempts to convert a solid fuel Aga to oil or gas using 'ad-hoc' parts could also raise safety issues and current legislation does not permit 'unapproved' gas burners or controls to be used. One owner who had moved house and recently bought a brand new Aga, explained to me how she now viewed her old, converted Aga which she had inherited and I thought she made a perfect analogy. 'You can put a motor on a bicycle but it will only ever be a motorised bicycle – it will never be a proper motorbike. Now I have bought a new Aga it is as though I have treated myself to a proper motorbike. Now my ovens do exactly what you say they should.' The other factor to be borne in mind is that of safety. Every new Aga has specific approvals from the appropriate official body. This applies for each variation in fuel, flue and number of ovens. Altering or modifying a product will nullify the approval and in the case of gas-fired cookers could be illegal. Because of the timeless design of an Aga, you could be paying thousands of pounds for a cooker that is already 40 or more years old, running on a fuel for which it was not designed. The best advice I can give is for you to obtain the 'Buying Used' leaflet from Aga so that you are aware of all the issues involved and you can therefore make an informed decision. Here are some of the clues to determine whether a cooker has been converted:

IDENTIFYING A CONVERTED COOKER

Does it say it is oil or gas fired anywhere on the cooker?

Look to see it if has lift-out circular plugs in the middle of the Boiling and Simmering Plates. If there are, it has been converted from solid fuel.

Are the oil or gas pipes taken into the cooker through the front burner door, with the pipes visible across the front plate of the cooker?

If there are, it has been converted from solid fuel.

Is the Aga front plate of the old 'Standard' design (pre-1973), but advertised as oil or gas?

If the heat indicator is not centrally above the Roasting Oven but further along, in the middle of the front plate, then the Aga has been converted from solid fuel.

BEFORE PURCHASING...

Here is a short list of the main questions you should be asking yourself so that you are able to make an informed purchasing decision:

- *How old is the cooker and how many owners have there been?*
- *Has the cooker been regularly serviced and is there proof of this?*
- *Is there a 5-year guarantee offered?*
- *Are the installers Aga-trained?*
- *What accessories and equipment are supplied with the cooker?*
- *What is the finish? Is it vitreous enamel or a paint or powder finish?*
- *Has the cooker been converted to run on a different fuel?*
- *Have parts been replaced or just cleaned and painted?*
- *Have genuine Aga parts been used to replace worn parts?*
- *Has the cooker got the appropriate mandatory approval?*
- *Will the cooker operate under automatic thermostatic control?*
- *Will the suppliers service the cooker?*
- *Are the engineers registered with the appropriate bodies?*

  CORGI for gas appliances – a legal requirement
  OFTEC for oil appliances
  HETAS for solid fuel appliances

- *Does the cooker contain asbestos products?*
- *Is there a charge for delivery?*
- *Will they deliver to your kitchen?*
- *Is there a charge for installation?*
- *Is the full range of Aga colours available?*
- *Is there a charge for different colours?*
- *Will the cooker be built in the home or delivered ready assembled?Aga cookers should only be moved in pieces and then hand-assembled in the home. They should never be moved in one piece as damage would almost certainly result.*

In 1994 the BBC Watchdog programme reported on converted Aga and Rayburn cookers.
The programme alerted potential purchasers about the problems and risks associated with buying a converted appliance. It reported that owners of converted Aga and Rayburn cookers were having a variety of problems from ignition difficulties to dangerous ventilation systems. They discovered that in some cases a new Aga could have been purchased for the same amount of money that customers were forced to spend in order to get the converted model modified and made safe.
If at all possible, even when fitting your Aga into an alcove, it is always a good idea to have some work surface on at least one side of the cooker.

PLANNING YOUR KITCHEN WITH AN AGA

This is invaluable for keeping a trivet for your Aga kettle, a dry wooden saltbox, jars of wooden spoons, etc. and also for putting heavy items emerging from the ovens. Have your work surfaces fitted to come right up to the side of the Aga top plate, and for preference, ever so slightly lower than the top plate. This means that things on the top plate will not catch on a raised edge, which they would otherwise. If you have a cupboard and drawer right next to the Aga you can keep laundered tea towels, etc, for a constant and handy supply of clean and dry linen. Use the dry cupboard for storing flour and sugar, etc., as there will be no danger of them becoming damp or caked. It is very important that if you are having tiles placed on the back wall behind your Aga, these are fitted before the cooker is installed. If tiles were positioned after the fitting of the top plate, they would need to be removed to provide access to internal parts with very probable damage. Try and fit in an airing space fitted with telescopic rails to the side of your Aga for hand and tea towels. This is also a good place to store the larger Aga oven accessories that won't fit in your kitchen cupboards, such as the full size roasting tins and plain shelves. It can be useful to have an extra small sink near your Aga which is handy for draining water when transferring vegetables to the Simmering Oven. The tap also comes in handy – once you've had this luxury it is sorely missed. Fitting a rail on the wall or ceiling above your Aga for hanging ironed shirts to air, and wet jackets to dry, can be a simple yet excellent laundry aid. A line of laundry can quickly be tidied away when guests are due. Depending on your style of kitchen, possibly consider installing an old-fashioned overhead pulley clothes airer, otherwise use an A-frame airer or old-fashioned clotheshorse for drying washing in front of the Aga overnight. You will save a lot on tumble dryer running costs. Make sure nothing could fall on to the closed Boiling Plate lid.

IRONING WHILE YOU SLEEP

The Aga is an airing cupboard in itself. The gentle but continuous warmth that is always given off is ideal for keeping tea towels and a hand towel dry on the rail. To air laundry safely, fold items up and place on top of the Simmering Plate lid. A word of caution, however: don't use the Boiling Plate lid or you will risk scorching. It is also important to make sure you don't cover the coil spring handle, otherwise it will become too hot when you try to lift it after removing the ironed washing. Everyday washing can even be fast-spun in the washing machine and then carefully shaken and folded before being placed on the closed lid. This is perfect for tea towels, pillow slips, t-shirts, children's everyday clothes, etc. and certainly cuts out a bulk of tiresome ironing. Turn items during the day when you are passing the cooker and replace with other garments. Pairs of jeans dry beautifully over the rail – turn around after an hour or so. If you are careful to avoid blocking air vents on the burner door on oil, gas and solid fuel models, sheets and duvet covers can be dried over the rail. It is best to use the right-hand side of the cooker for this, in front of the oven doors.

MORE THAN JUST A COOKER

Your local Aga Specialist will be able to give you details of exact running costs for your Aga. When you take into account all the different things that it will do for you, and the savings on not having to use other equipment, you will find that the Aga is the most economical cooker in the world. Remember, you no longer need to run up bills using any of the following: an electric kettle, frying pan, toaster, slow cooker or crockpot, crêpe-maker, sandwich toaster, steamer, yoghurt maker, bread machine or popcorn maker – the list goes on and on.... Certainly in my house I find I have no need for using an expensive tumble dryer. I also turn on the central heating much later in the season than most people, and again off in the spring quite a few weeks earlier. After its famous cooking abilities, I think it is the sheer presence of an Aga in the kitchen and its constant warmth that makes it so useful. Whether bringing a bottle of wine to room temperature after being brought from the cellar, to drying out the paper that has become soaked in the letterbox, Aga owners never stop finding new uses for the gentle warmth given off by their cooker.

PERSONAL AGA TECHNIQUE AUDIT

If you've made it this far, you should now be instinctively adopting Aga cooking principles. In the table below, the first column lists some practices which are wasteful of the Aga's stored heat. Some suggested better techniques are listed in the right column. Work your way down the left side of the table and see if you can suggest a remedy for each bad practice, before checking the right to see how you did. If you need to, re-visit each relevant section to make sure you fully understand suitable Aga positionings and techniques.

Bad Aga Practice	Good Aga Practice
Boiling potatoes and vegetables for the whole time on the hotplates	Steam potatoes and vegetables in the Simmering Oven
Bad Aga Practice Softening onions for long periods on the Simmering Plate	**Good Aga Practice** Soften onions in the Simmering Oven and then return to the hotplates
Bad Aga Practice Sautéing or frying meat for prolonged periods on the Boiling Plate	**Good Aga Practice** Sauté or fry meat in a pan and transfer to the floor of the Roasting Oven or use a roasting tin on the floor of the Roasting Oven
Bad Aga Practice Simmering Bolognaise and Ragù sauces on the Simmering Plate	**Good Aga Practice** Simmer Bolognaise and Ragù sauces in the Simmering Oven
Bad Aga Practice Frying a lot of food on the Boiling and Simmering Plates	**Good Aga Practice** Fry large quantities of food on the floor of the Roasting Oven
Bad Aga Practice Using tiered steamers for vegetables on the Simmering Plate for a long period	**Good Aga Practice** Use the Simmering Oven for root vegetables and steam green vegetables on the Boiling Plate or Simmering Plate

Bad Aga Practice	Good Aga Practice
Bad Aga Practice Steaming puddings for hours on the Simmering Plate	**Good Aga Practice** Steam puddings for hours in the Simmering Oven
Bad Aga Practice Using saucepans with very poor bases or having concentric rings	**Good Aga Practice** Use only saucepans with thick and perfectly flat bases
Bad Aga Practice Simmering stock on the Simmering Plate for several hours	**Good Aga Practice** Simmer stock in the Simmering Oven for several hours or overnight
Bad Aga Practice Reducing sauces with prolonged boiling on the Boiling Plate	**Good Aga Practice** Reduce sauces with prolonged boiling on the floor of the Roasting Oven
Bad Aga Practice Simmering bacon and gammon joints on the Simmering Plate	**Good Aga Practice** Simmer bacon and gammon joints in the Simmering Oven
Bad Aga Practice Placing coins on the Simmering Plate 'to make it cook more slowly'	**Good Aga Practice** Dead slow simmering is best achieved in the Simmering Oven and saves wasting heat
Bad Aga Practice Placing containers of cold water into the Roasting Oven to attempt to cool it down before baking a rich fruit cake	**Good Aga Practice** Understand the use of the cold plain shelf and the Simmering Oven rich fruit cake method
Bad Aga Practice Leaving kettles on the Simmering Plate to attempt to reduce the Roasting Oven temperature when baking cakes	**Good Aga Practice** Select the correct heat zone and use cold plain shelves if necessary or transfer the cake to finish cooking in the Simmering Oven
Bad Aga Practice Attempting to make gravy on the Boiling Plate using an Aga roasting tin	**Good Aga Practice** If making gravy in an Aga roasting tin, use the Simmering Plate or the floor of the Roasting Oven to prevent the tin from warping

THE 2 OVEN AGA

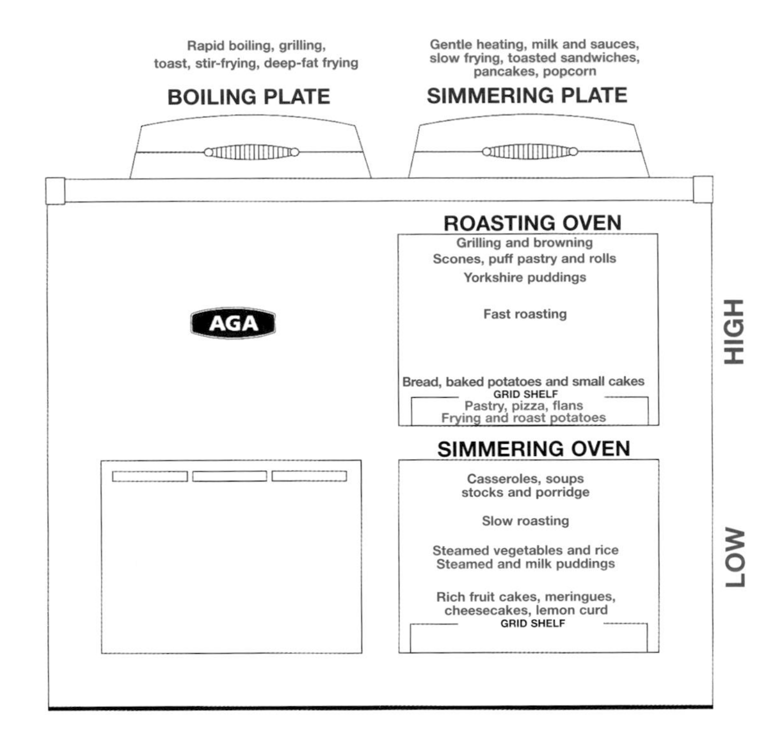

THE 3 OVEN AGA

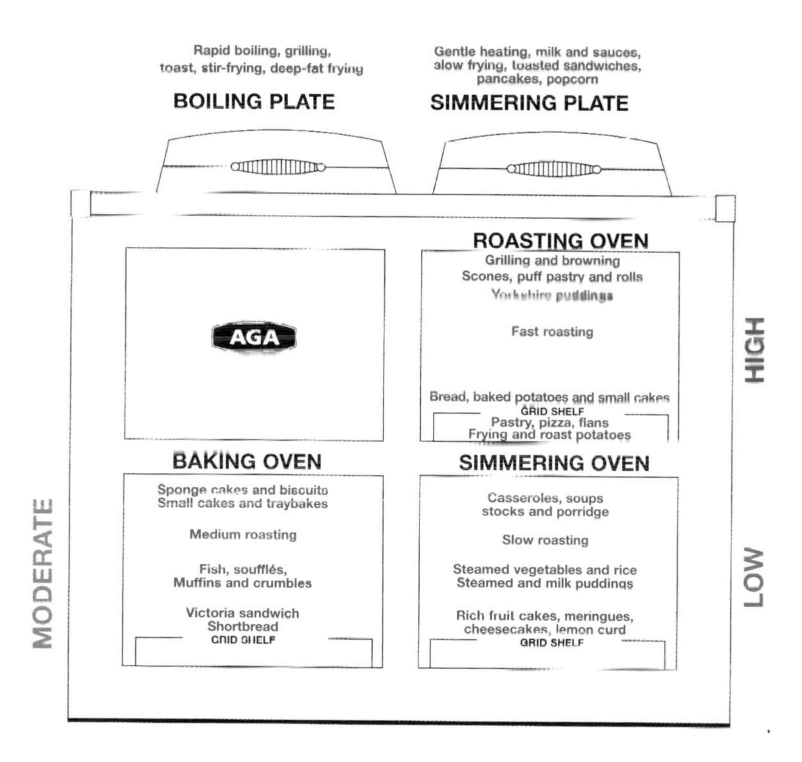

THE 4 OVEN AGA

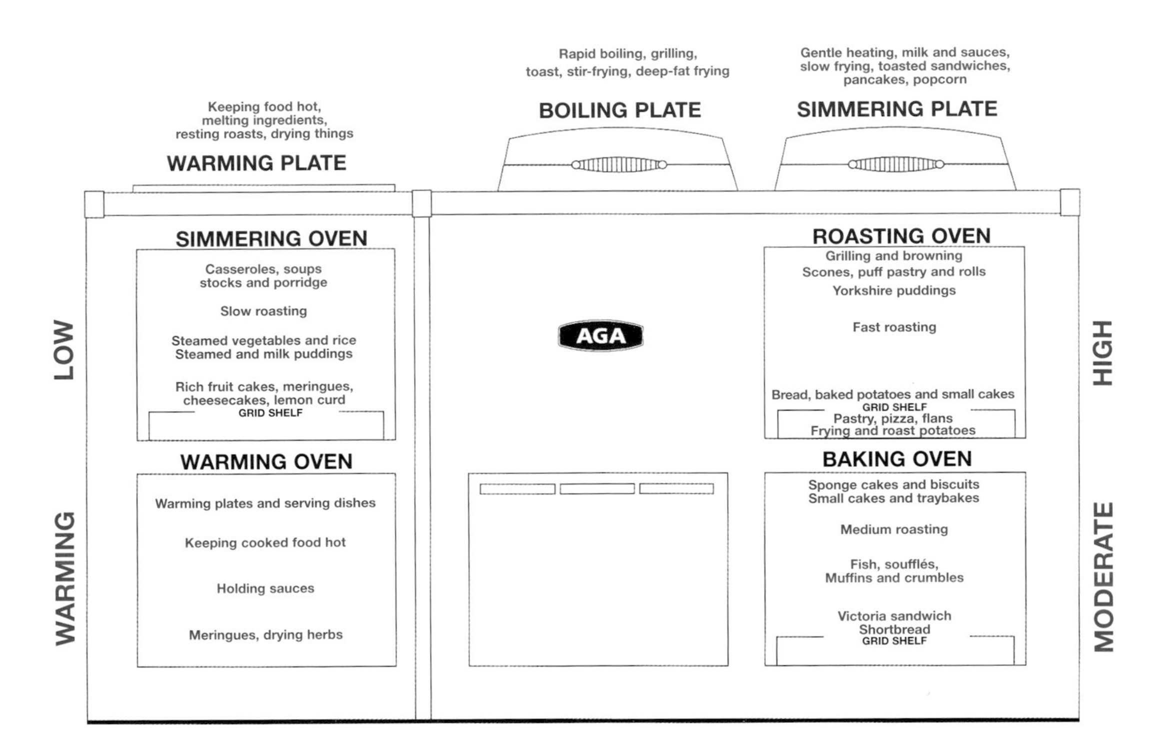

ACKNOWLEDGEMENTS

My thanks to all my family, friends, colleagues, fellow chefs and, of course, Aga owners everywhere for their constant support and encouragement. A special thanks to Ken, Carwen and Pete for their tireless help in meeting publishing deadlines. To everyone at Aga-Rayburn, it is a pleasure to continue to work with such an enthusiastic group of people. Also, a huge thank you to my publisher, Jon Croft, editor Meg Avent and graphic designer, Matt Inwood at Absolute Press, who are the best people in the world to write a book with. They have helped make this book a really enjoyable project.

AGA is a registered trademark of Aga Foodservice Group plc.

BAKE-O-GLIDE™ is a re-usable non-stick coated cooking material, available from all Aga Specialists.

The Aga Cook *Aide-mémoires* have been developed from an idea used with kind permission of Aga-Rayburn.

ABOUT THE AUTHOR

A dynamic and accomplished chef, Richard is an authority on Aga cookery. He has helped many thousands of Aga owners to get the very best out of their cookers. As well as having featured on TV and radio, he writes for several magazines and contributes a regular column to the official Aga Magazine. A best-selling author, he is also the resident Aga cookery expert, The Cookery Doctor, with the award-winning Agalinks website at www.agalinks.com. Since its launch four years ago, he has answered more than three thousand Aga enquiries, making him the world's No 1 online Aga expert. This is his sixth book.

INDEX